beach

THIS IS A HOLY WATER TITLE

www.holy-water.co.uk

First Edition published by Holy Water Limited
Limited edition of 2000

ISBN 0-9548238-0-X

Printed in Dubai

A few months after he had settled in I hopped on a ferry and paid him a visit. During the nights we'd walk around from pub to pub, meeting people along the way, making new friends, exchanging stories, sharing in the traditions that island people have been for centuries. But he made his living as a busker, playing music on the streets for money, so during the days I was left to my own devices while he rattled out folk and blues tunes on his Dobro and harmonica for the folks in the shopping district to enjoy.

One afternoon I decided to visit a rocky beach that we had eyed from the bus earlier in the week and that he had told me I must visit before I left to go back to the mainland. I've always been drawn to the ocean and enjoy the rewards that come from walking down a beach alone, picking up small treasures along the way. As I combed this particular one, which faced west out into the Pacific and was being pounded by some fairly serious waves, I kept finding these amazing little stones that appeared to me to be gems of all different colors. Green, blue, beige, opaque, I even found a few orange and red ones. All different shapes, most were smooth around the edges yet they had a slightly rough texture, as though they'd been buffed with fine-grained sandpaper. I collected a handful which turned into a couple of pocketfuls which turned into searching for a plastic bag to fill up half way with these priceless stones. After many hours of collecting I eventually returned back to the house to show my friend the riches that we were going to exchange for many ales.

When I got to the house he was rolling a cigarette out on the front stoop. I showed him the bag of loot and while he was glad that I had collected it he laughed when I asked about the prospect of getting any money for it. He informed me that it was simply beach glass: pieces of glass bottles that have been broken somewhere along the line and washed ashore. Over years of washing from shore to shore, the edges of those pieces of glass gain a new texture, are less rough and they take on a new form, one that's arguably better than their previous one.

We talked that night about the obvious metaphors in beach glass. About our lives and about how the experiences that we take with us help to shape and mold us into the people we are, much like those waves and rocks do to the glass.

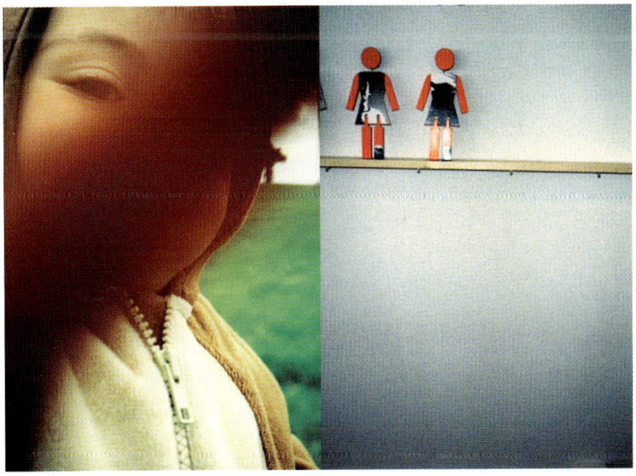

A few years ago I moved to Los Angeles and since my arrival have shot many photographs of the people, places and things that I've come across while exploring the city. I have yet to find any real beach glass on the sandy beaches of this locale but the things I've seen and the people whom I've met here have helped to round my edges and turn me into the person who I am today; the photographs you are about to view in the following pages are a part of my personal collection of beach glass from the past three years, much like the contents of that plastic bag that I brought home to my friend on that day so many years ago. The book is the bag, the photos the beach glass, you are that friend who moved to the island and the only difference is that these pieces are more priceless to me than anything in the world.

This book is dedicated to that friend, Jason Donaldson, who has been an inspiration to me in too many ways to count. Thanks, Jason.

Bob Kronbauer, Los Angeles, 2004
bobk@crownfarmer.com

6

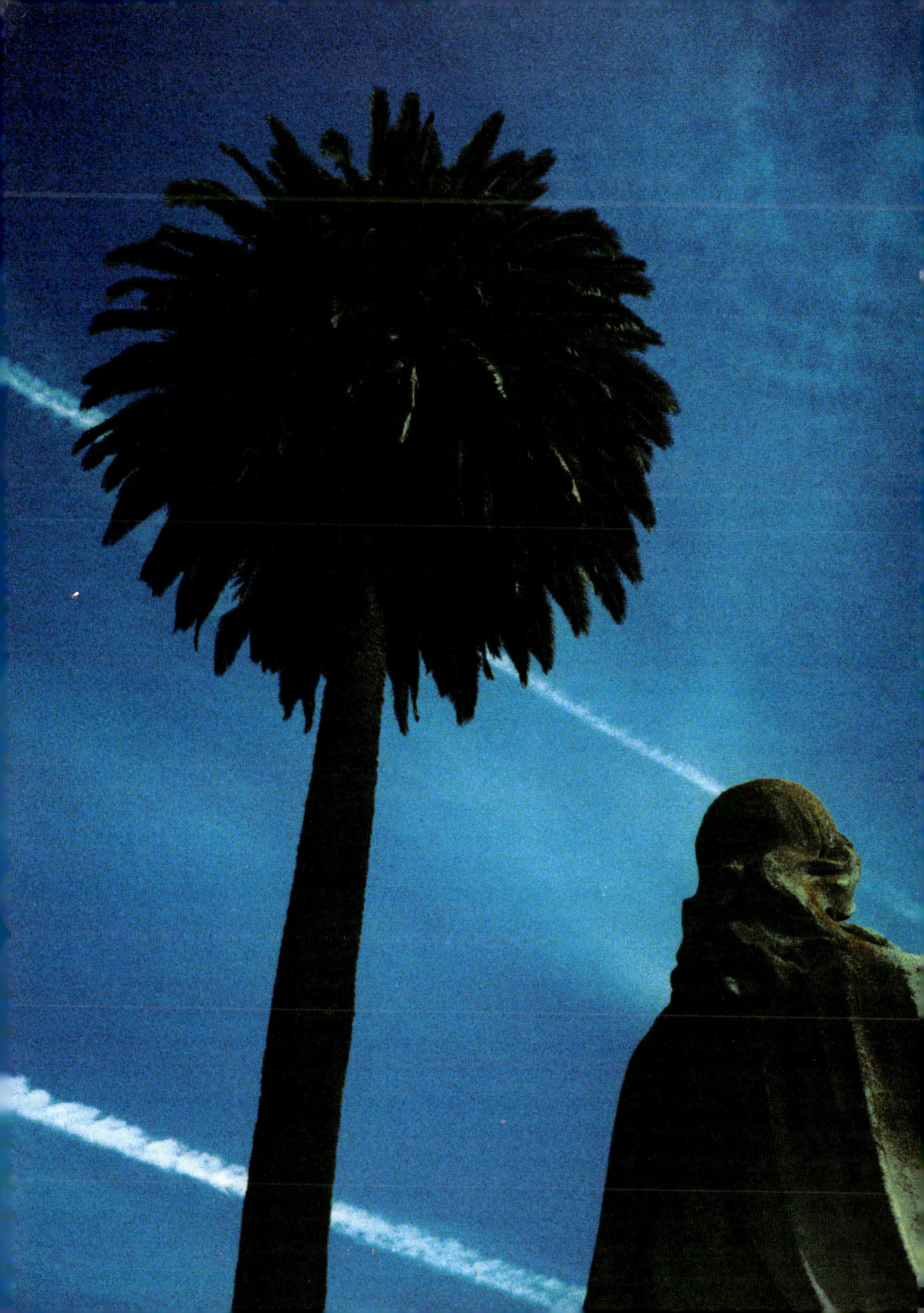

8

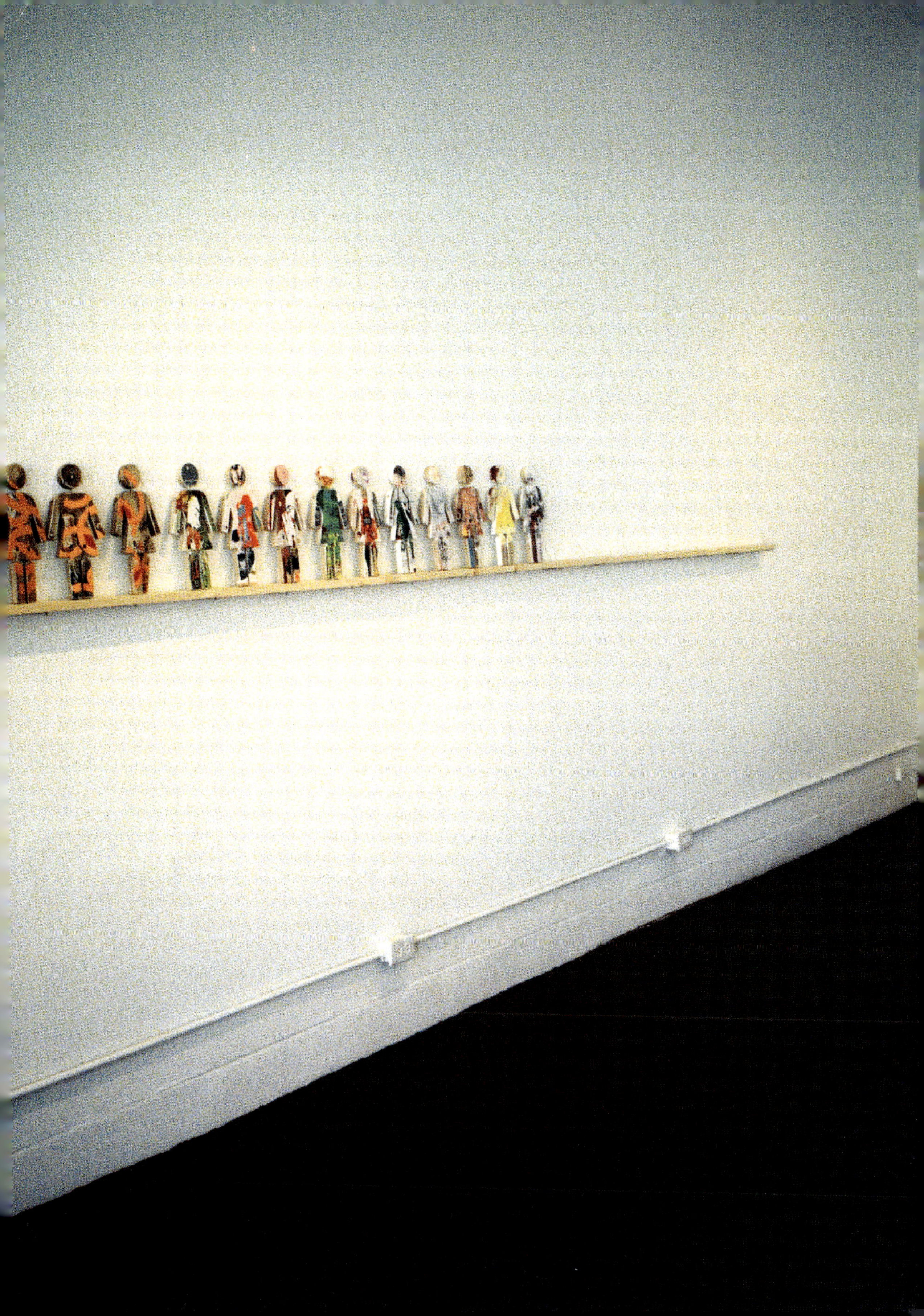

10

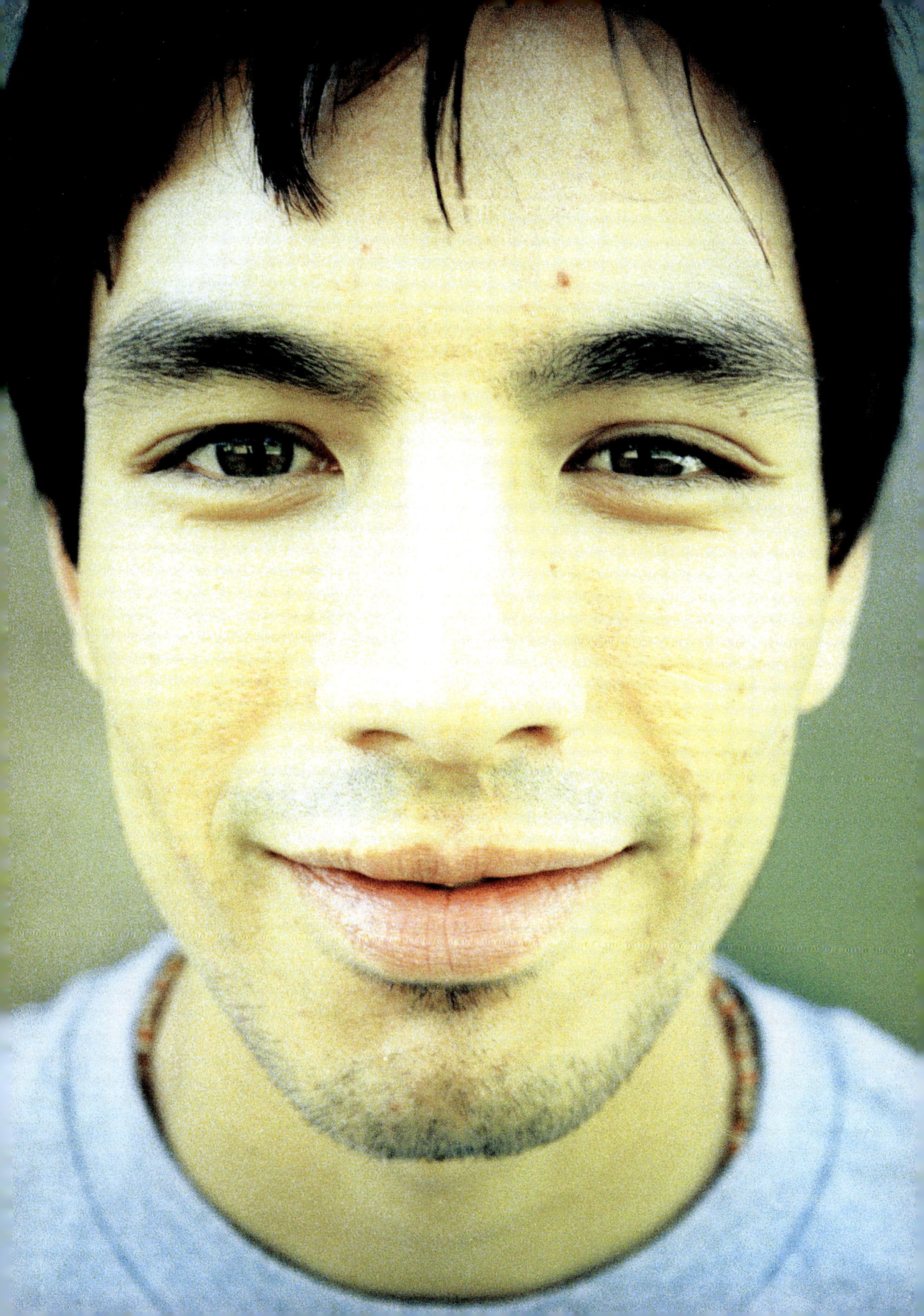

12

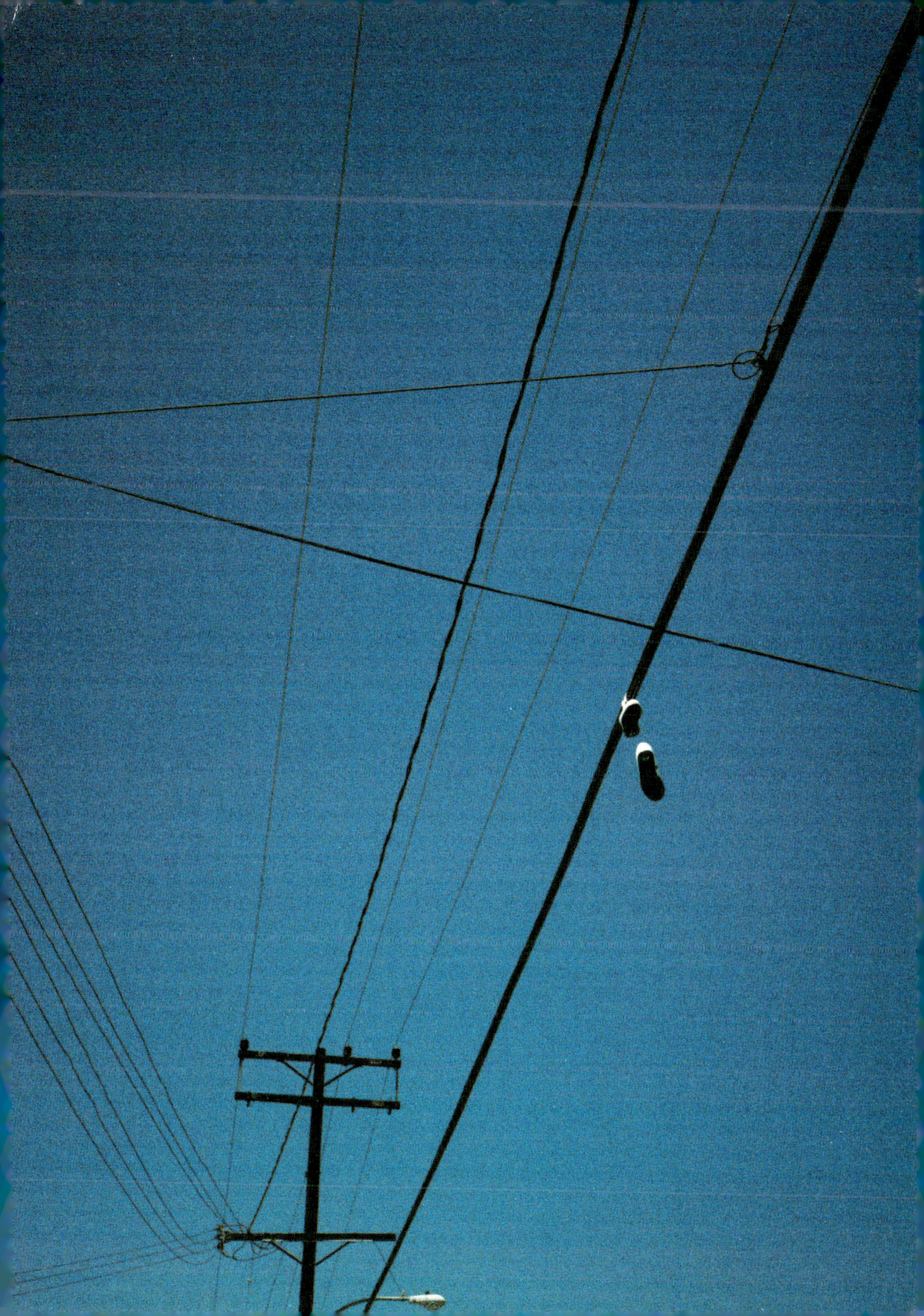

14

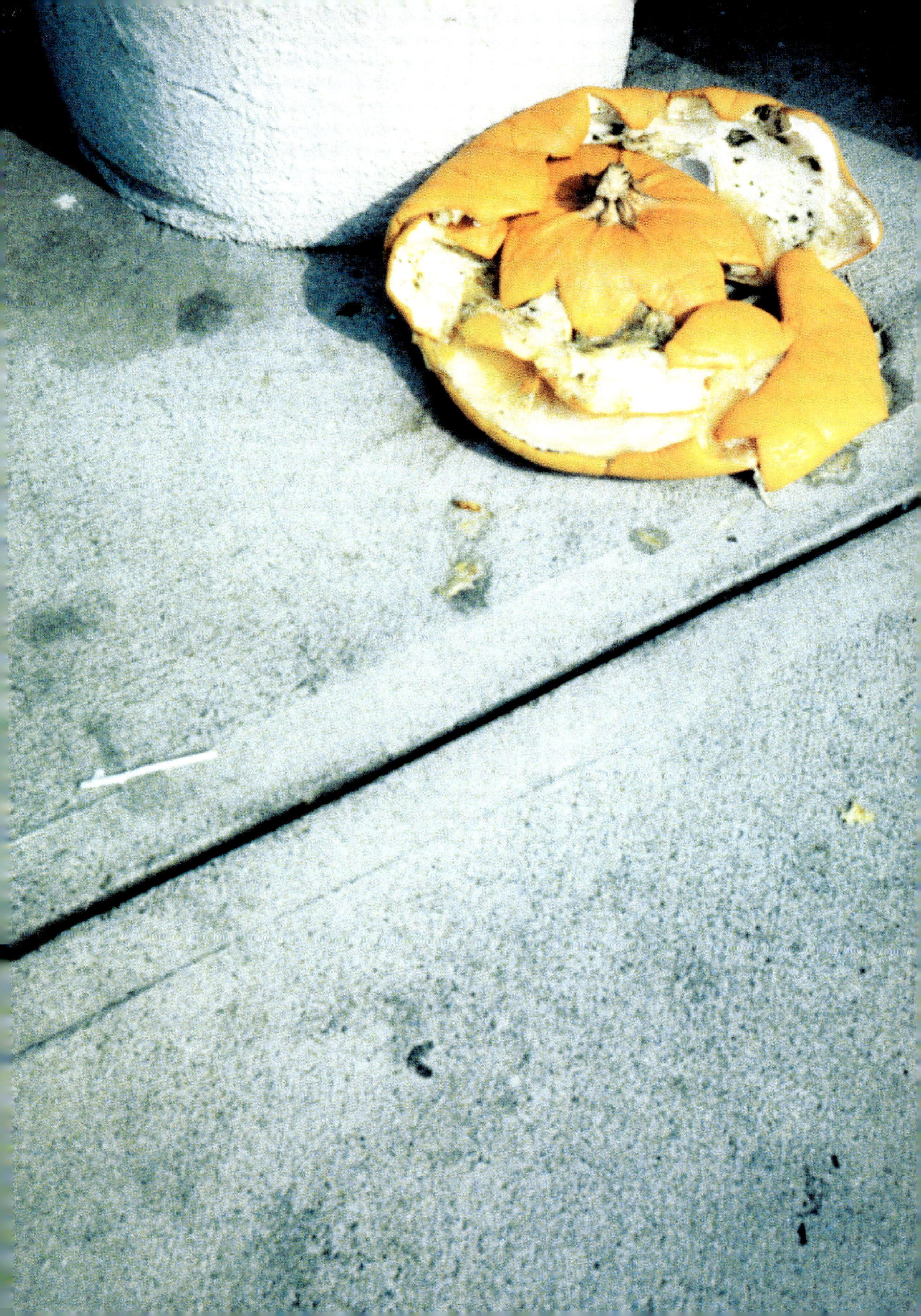

16

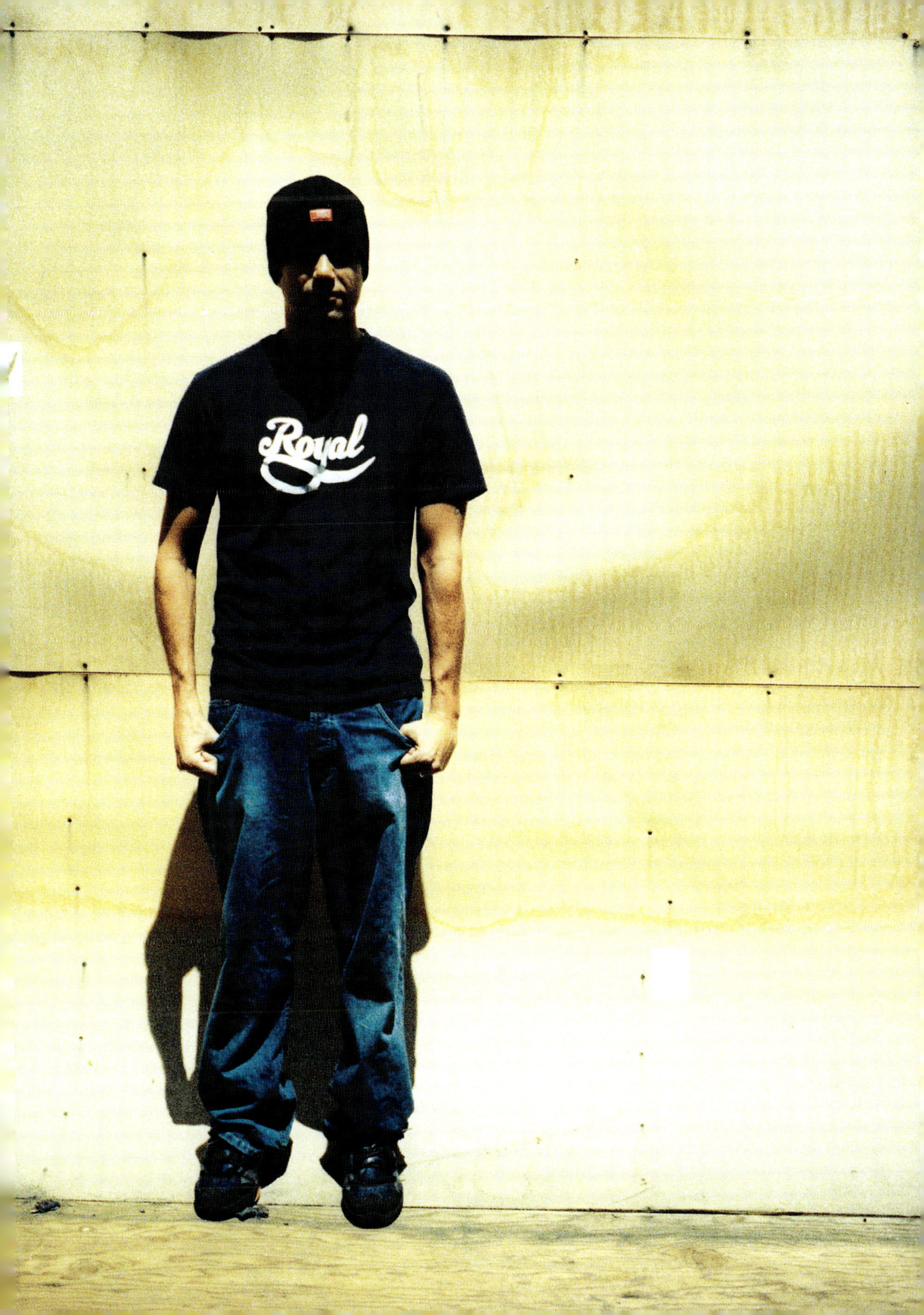
Royal

18

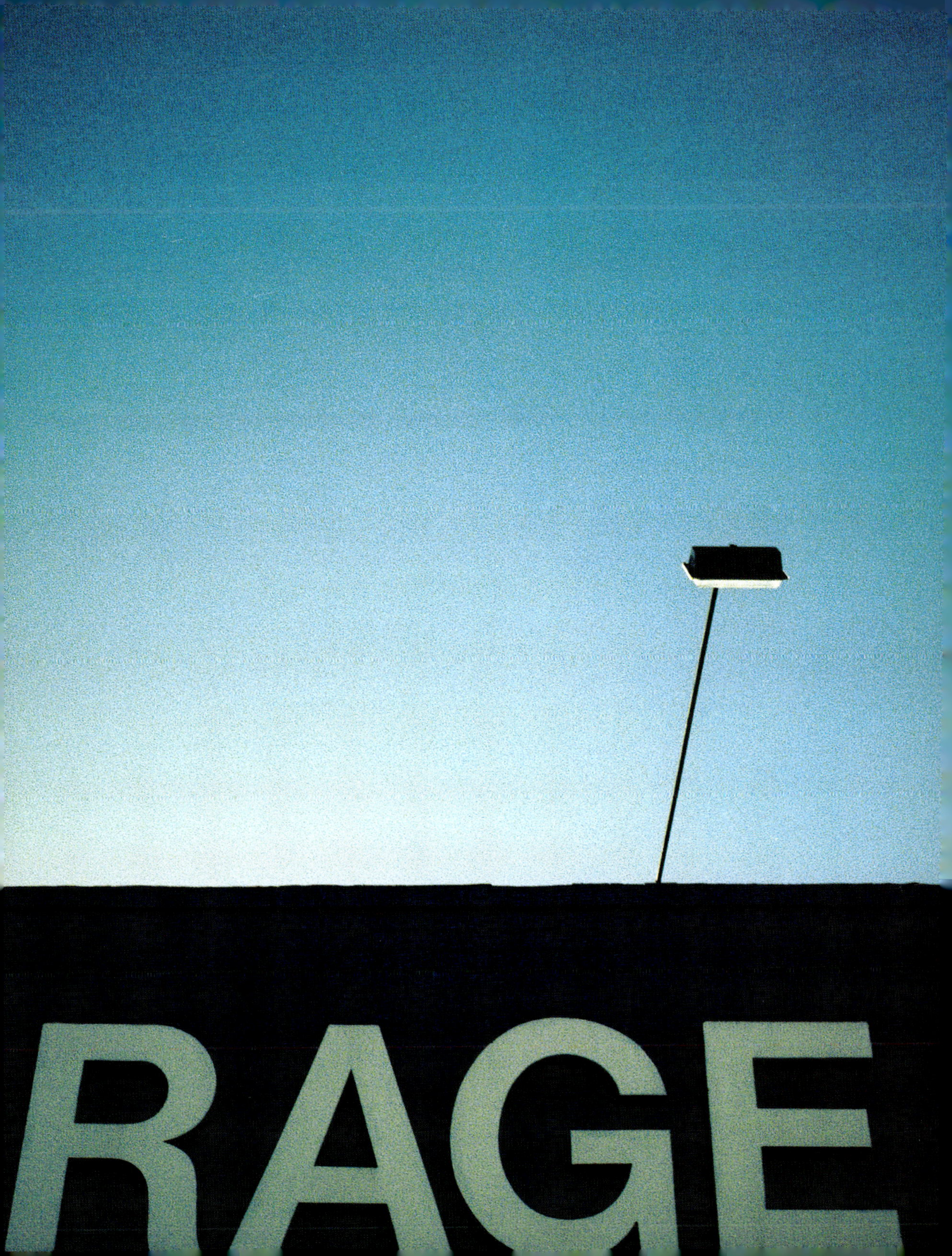
RAGE

20

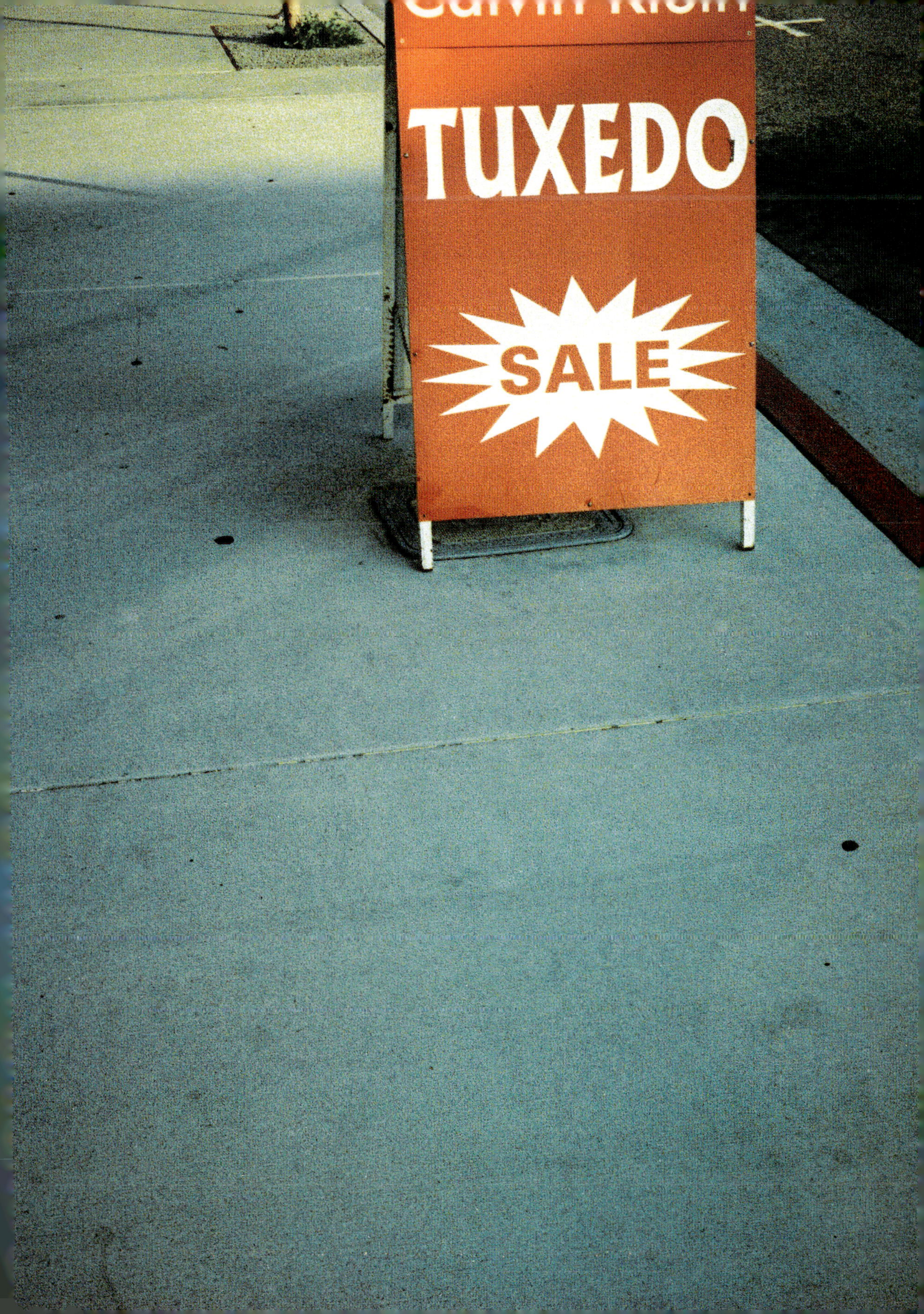
TUXEDO
SALE

22

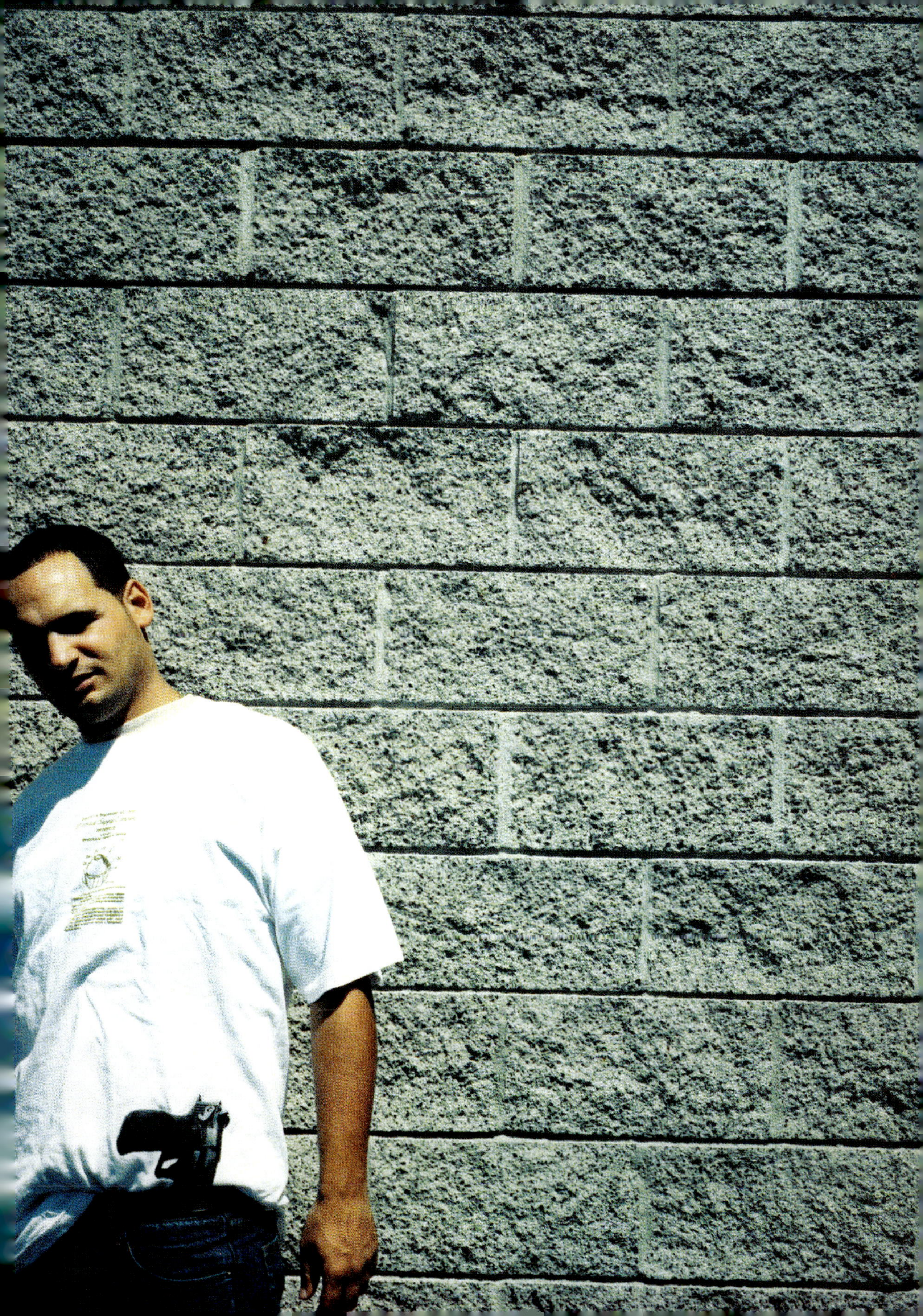

26

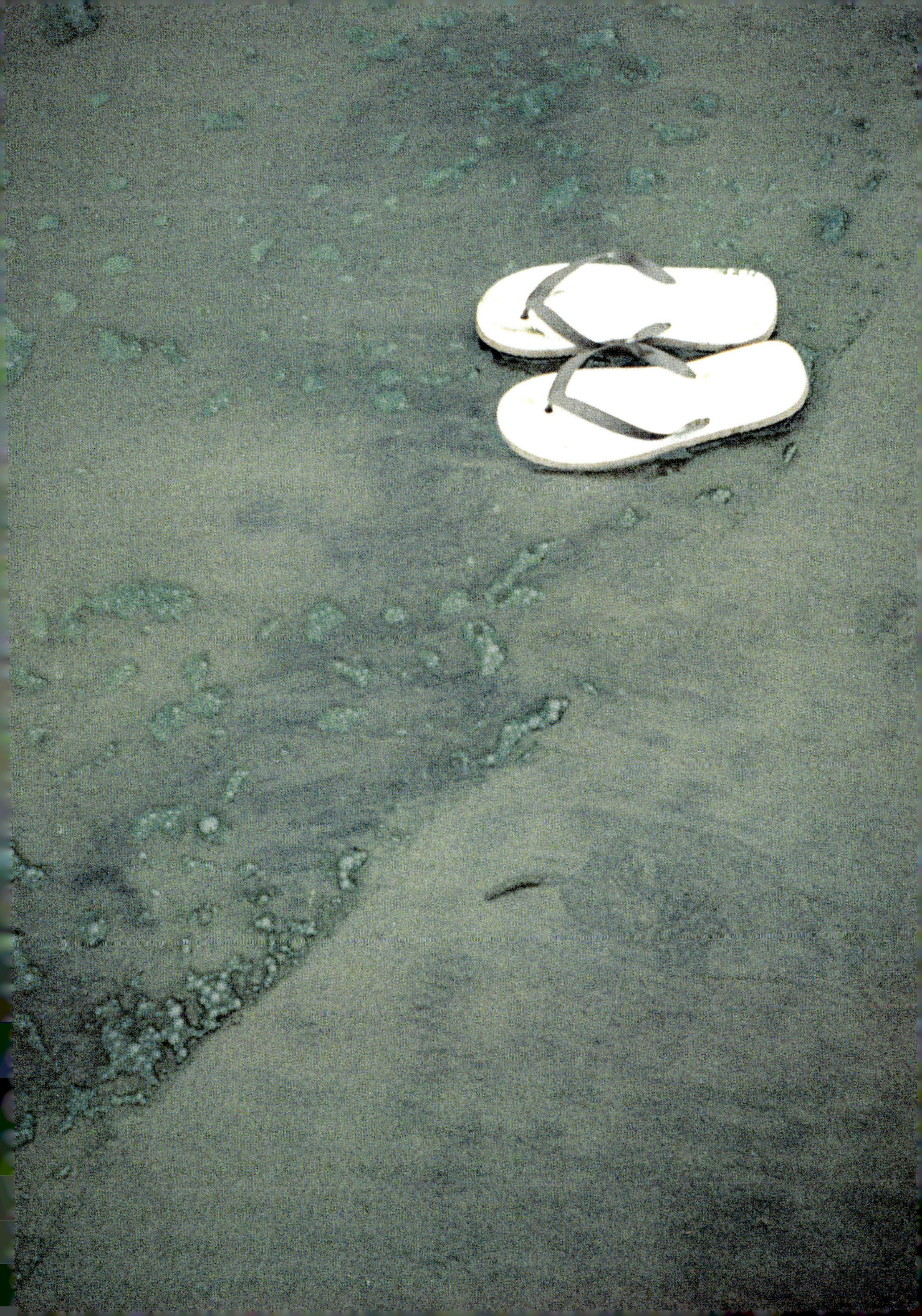

28

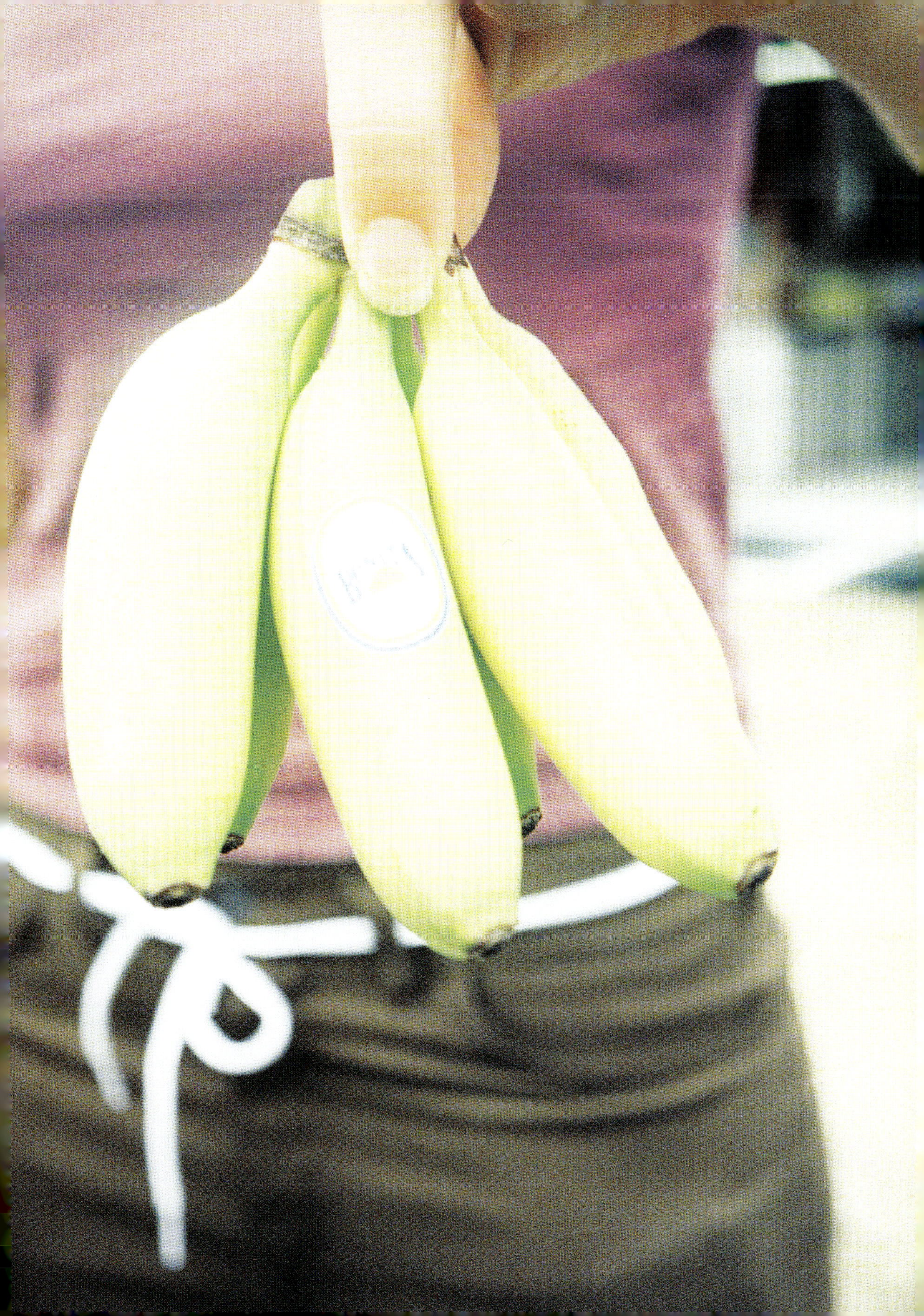

30

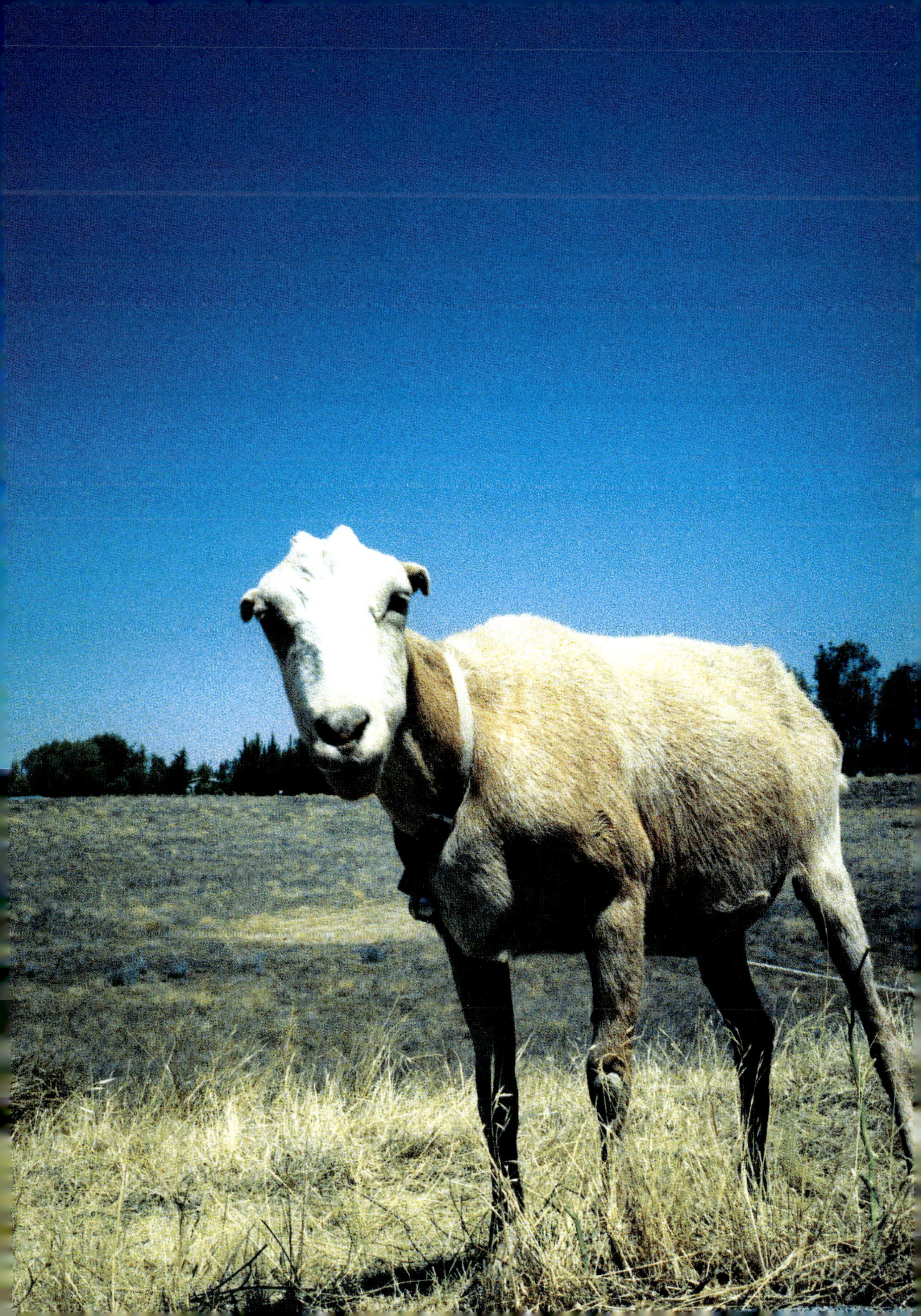

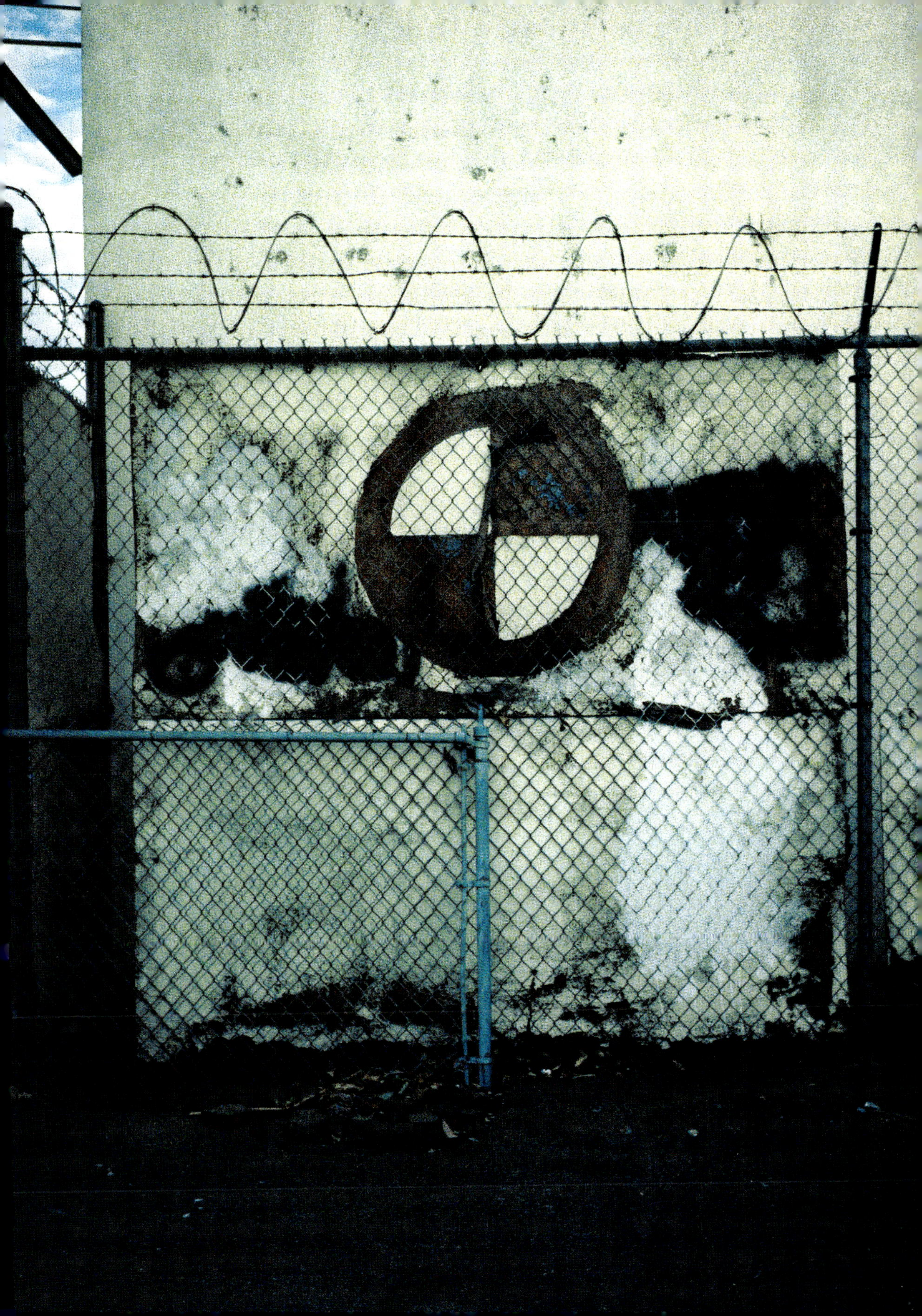

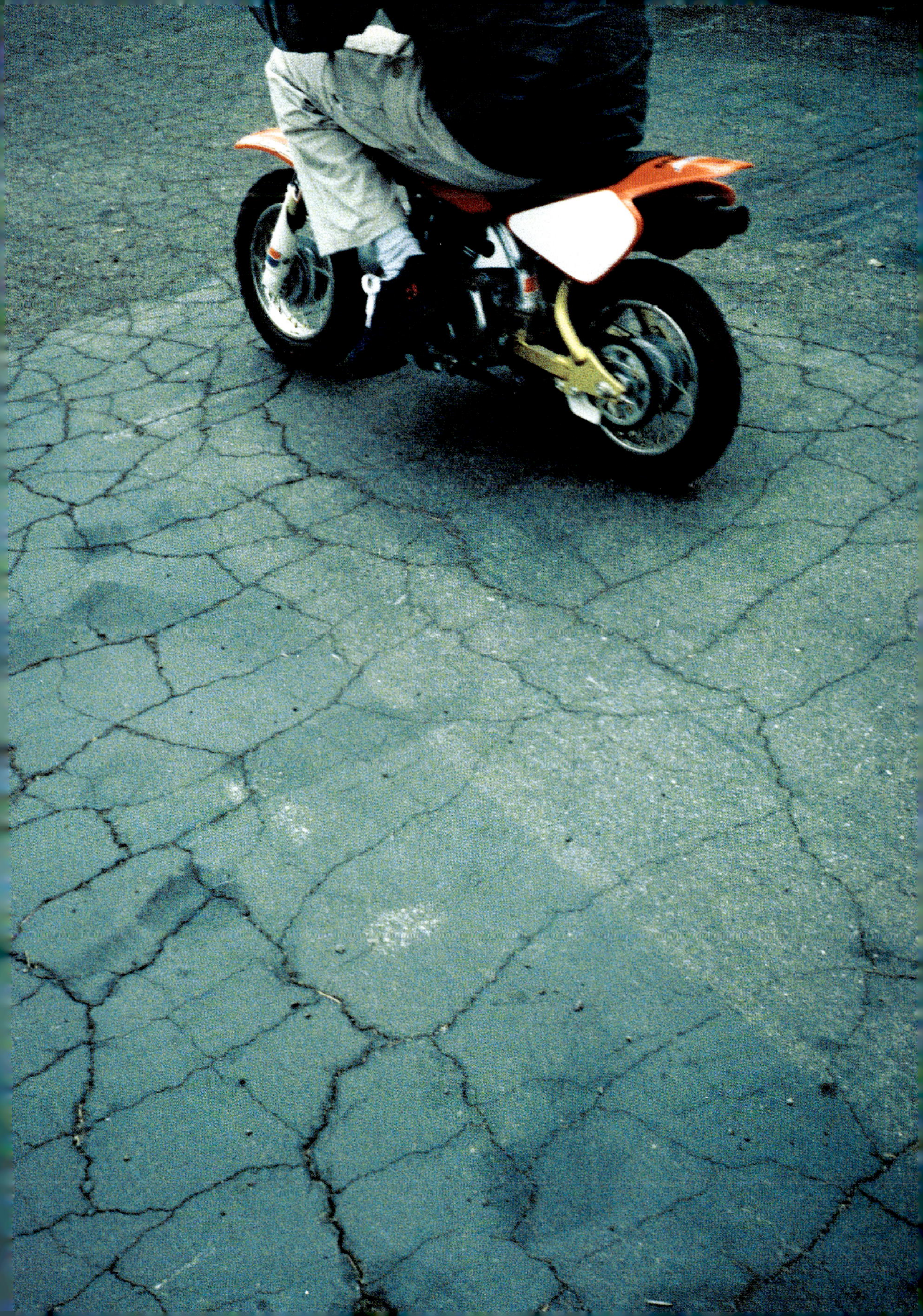

36

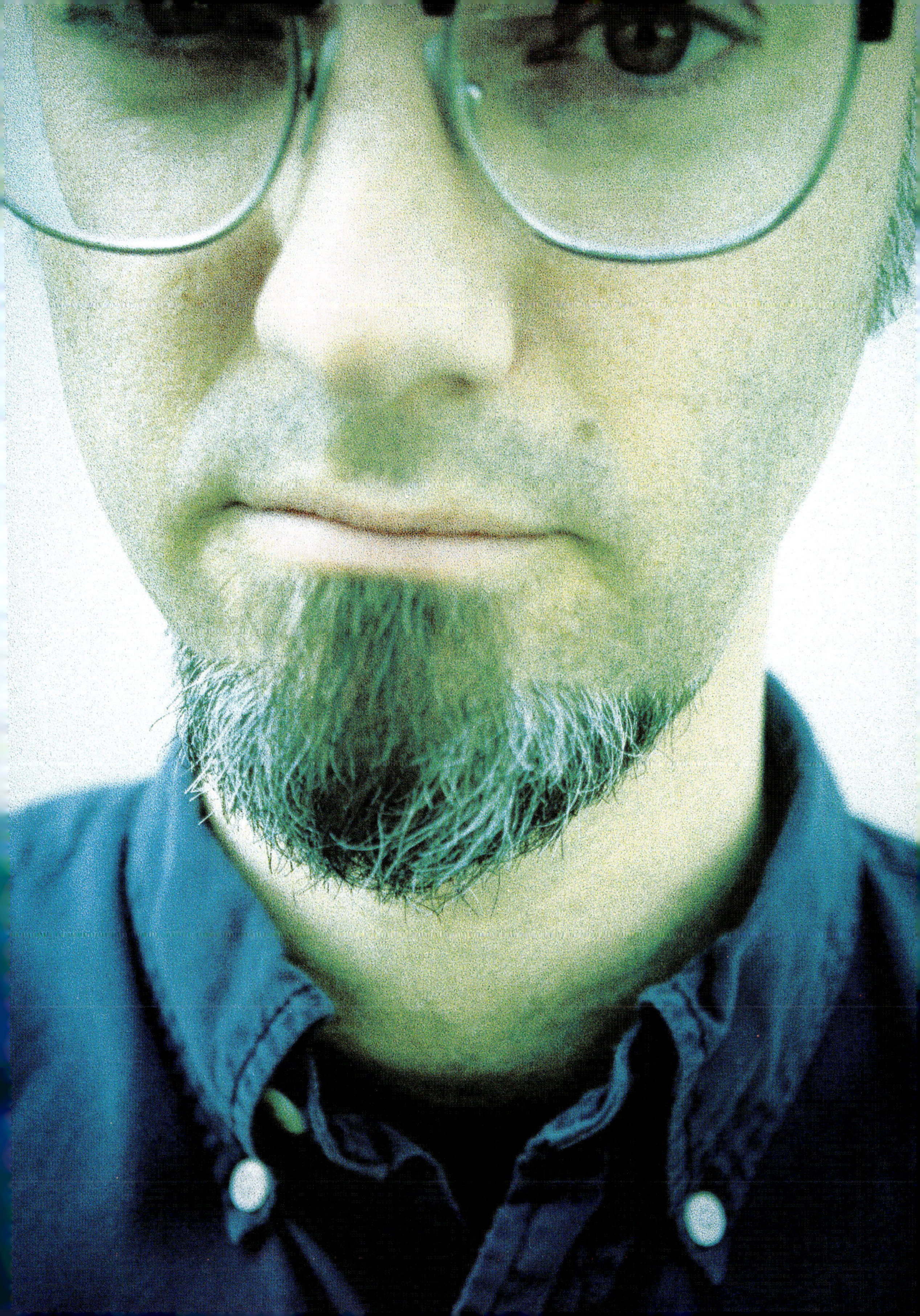

38

40

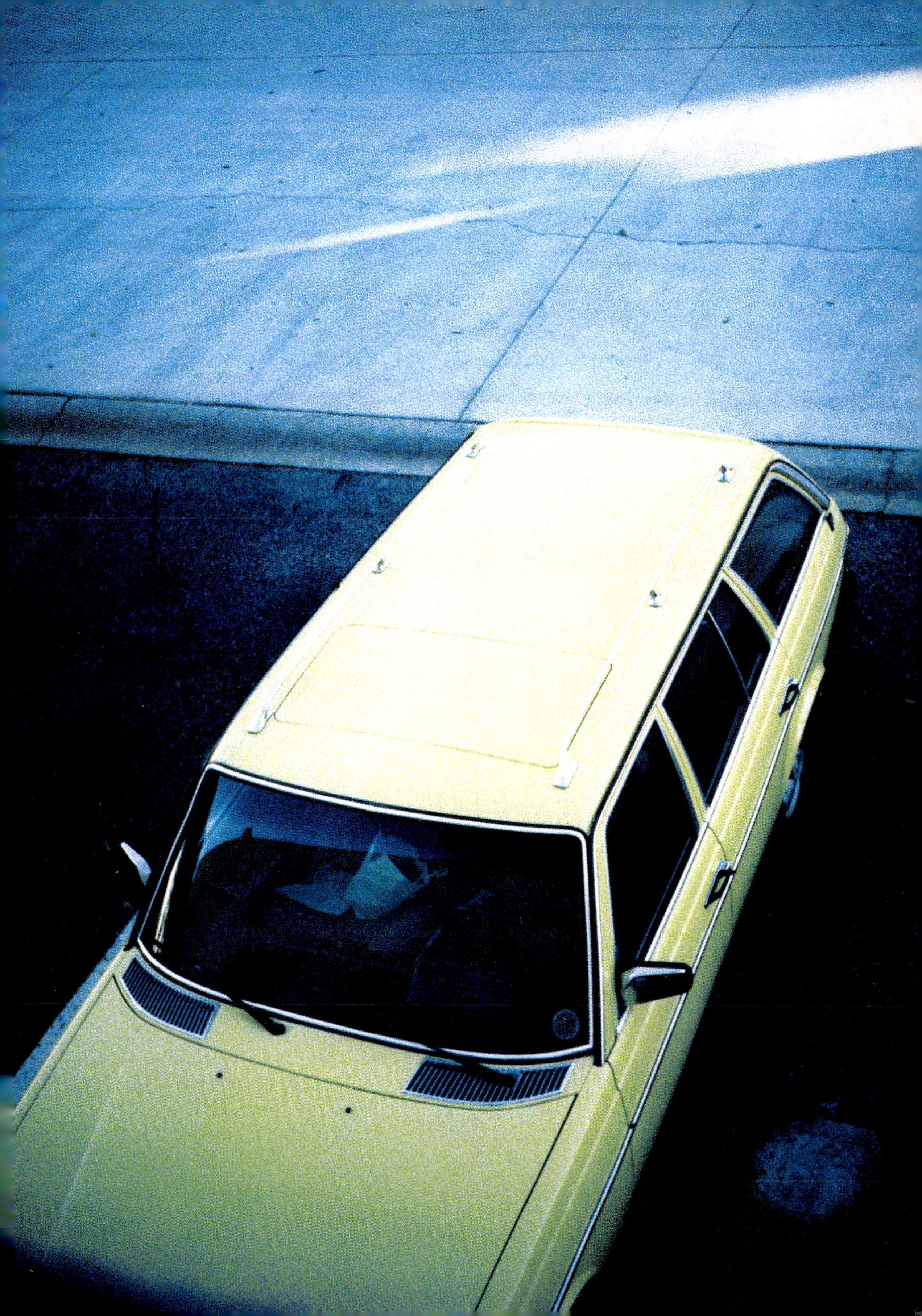

42

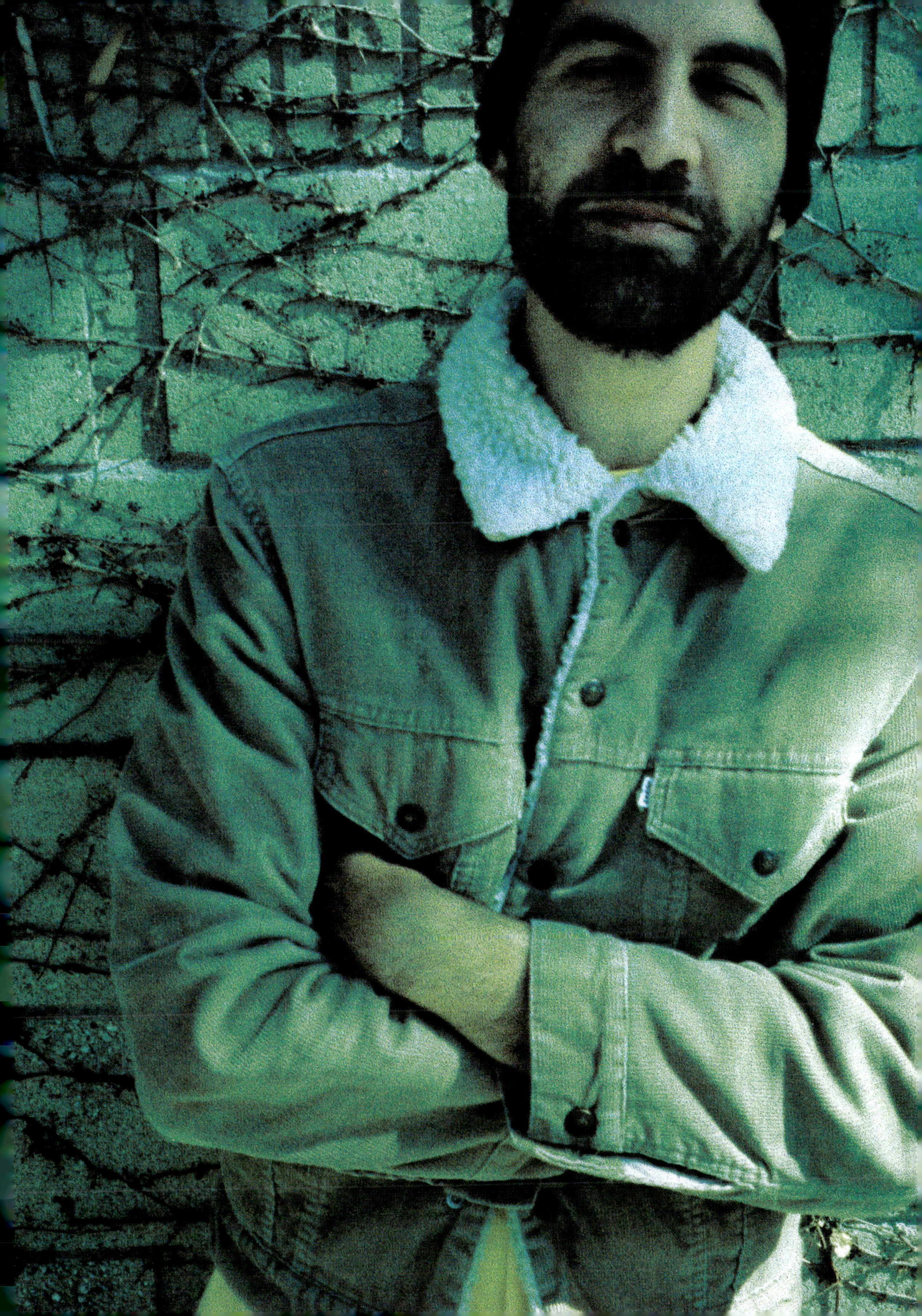

44

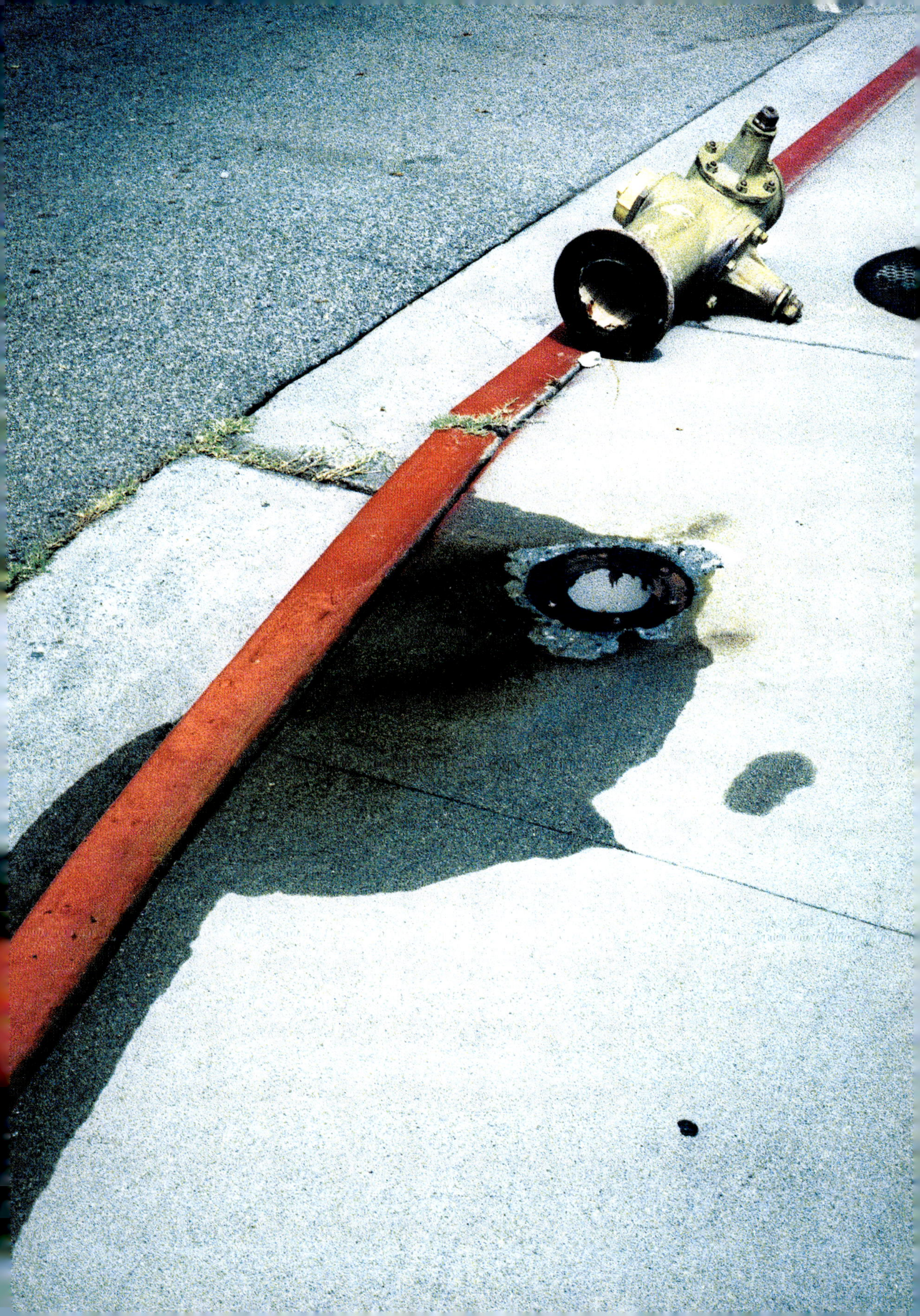

46

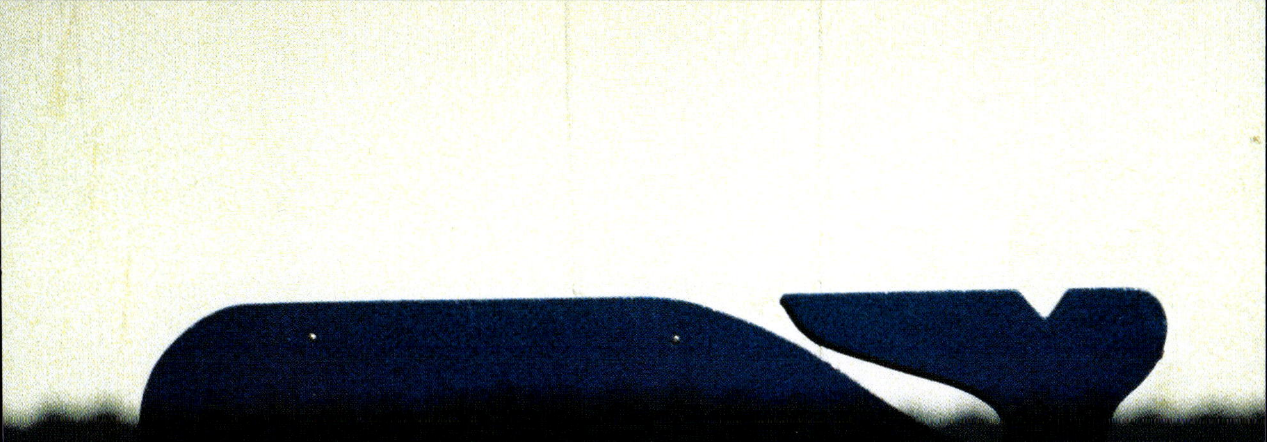

48

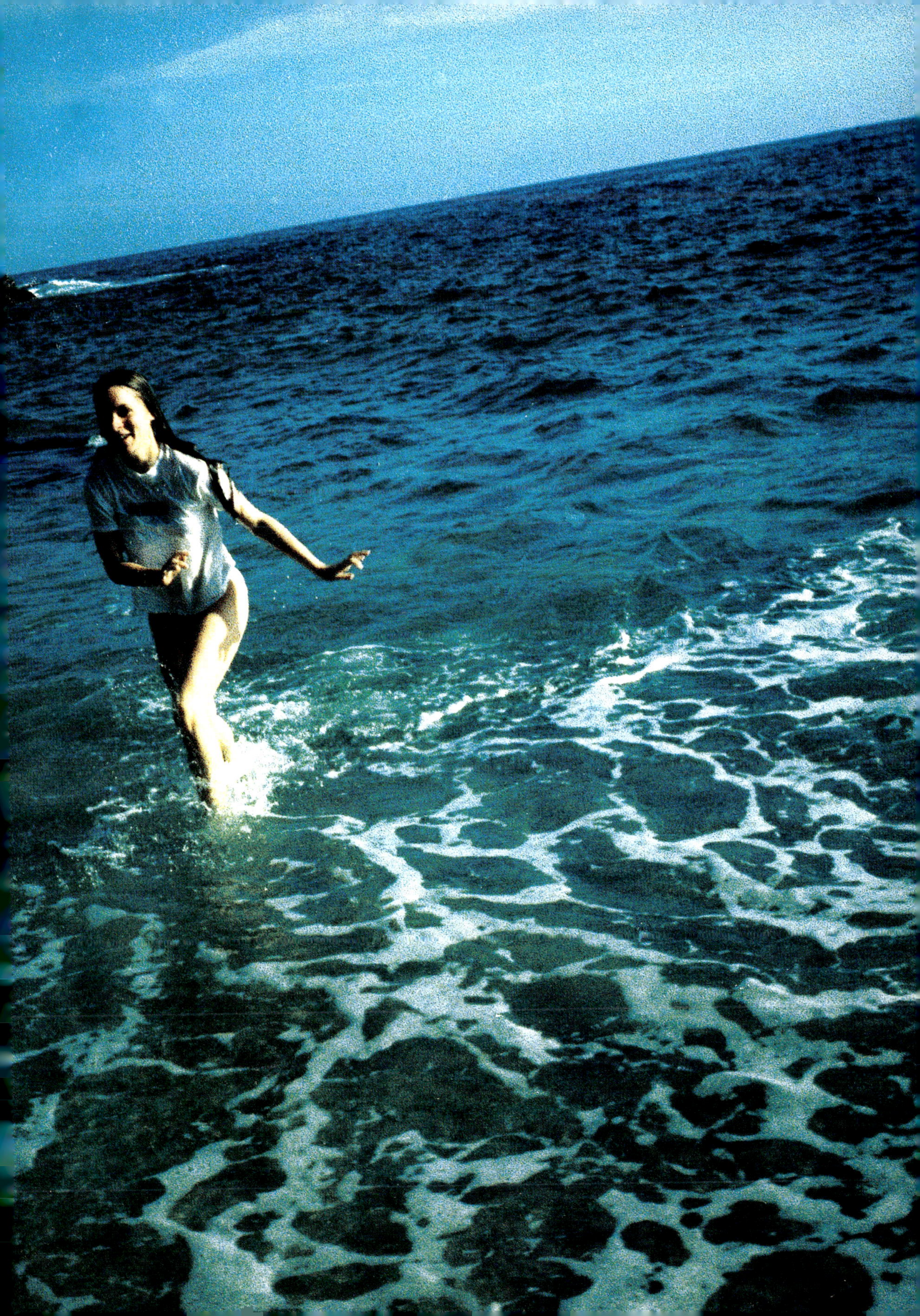

50

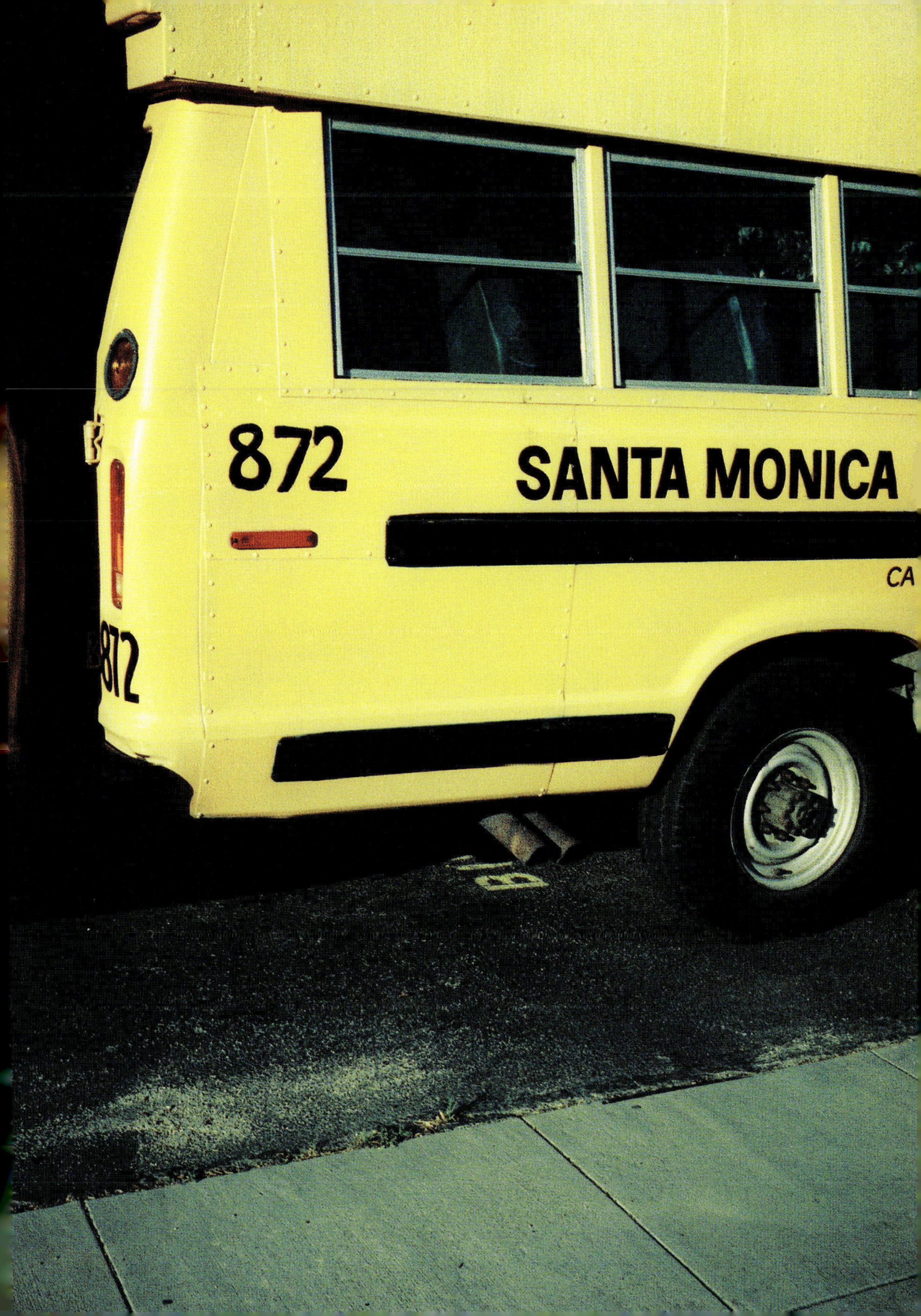
872
SANTA MONICA
CA
872

52

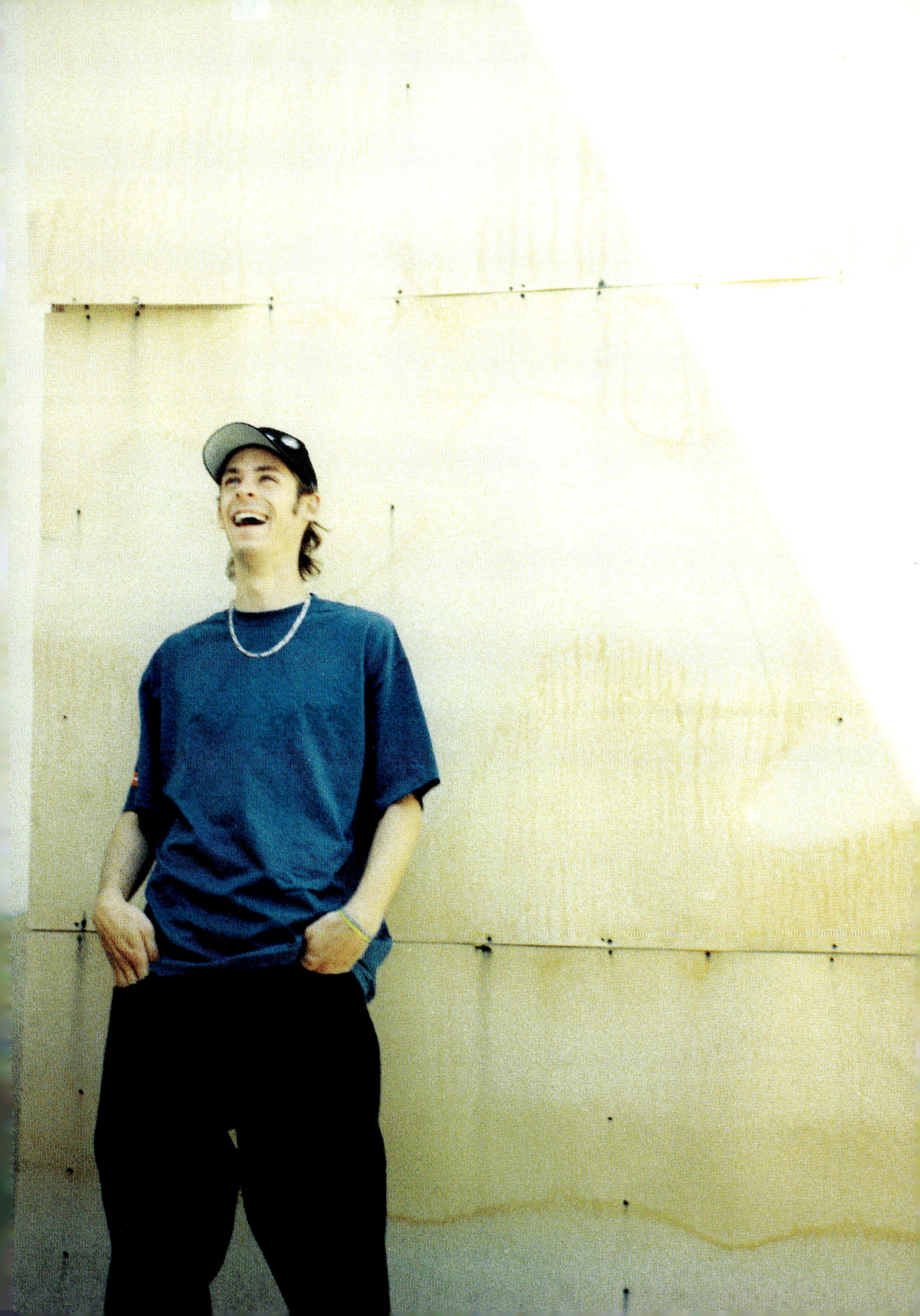

56

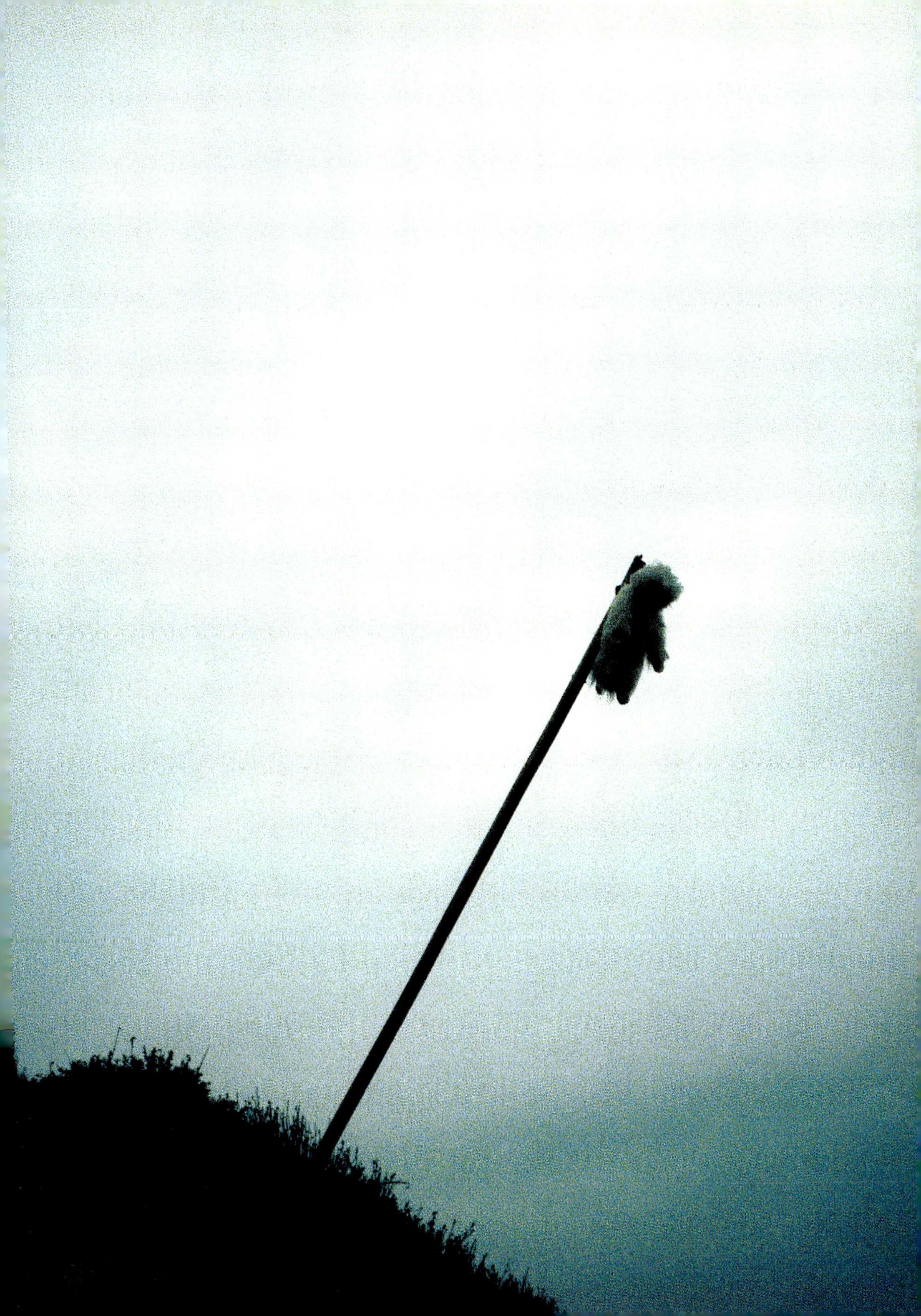

58

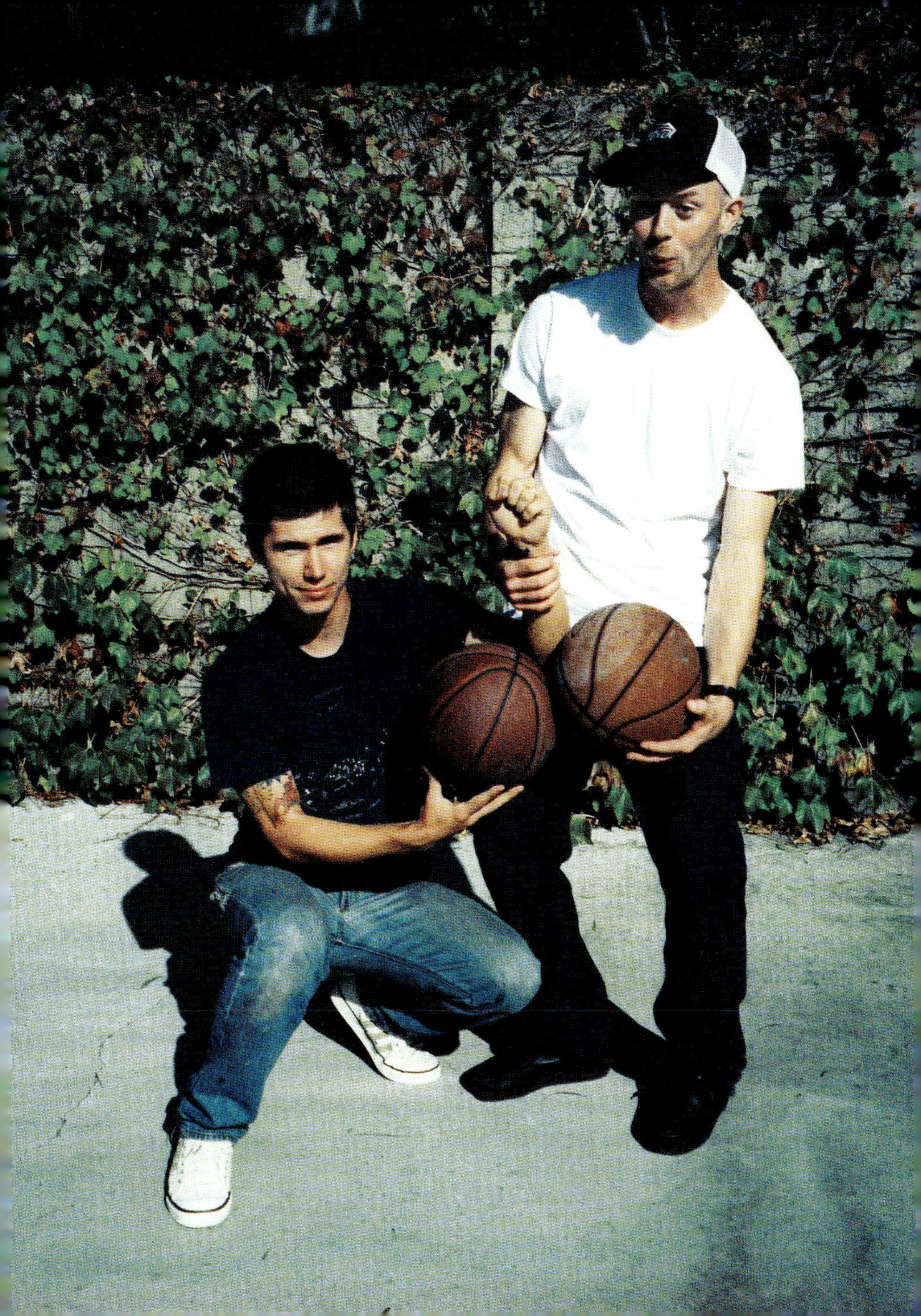

60

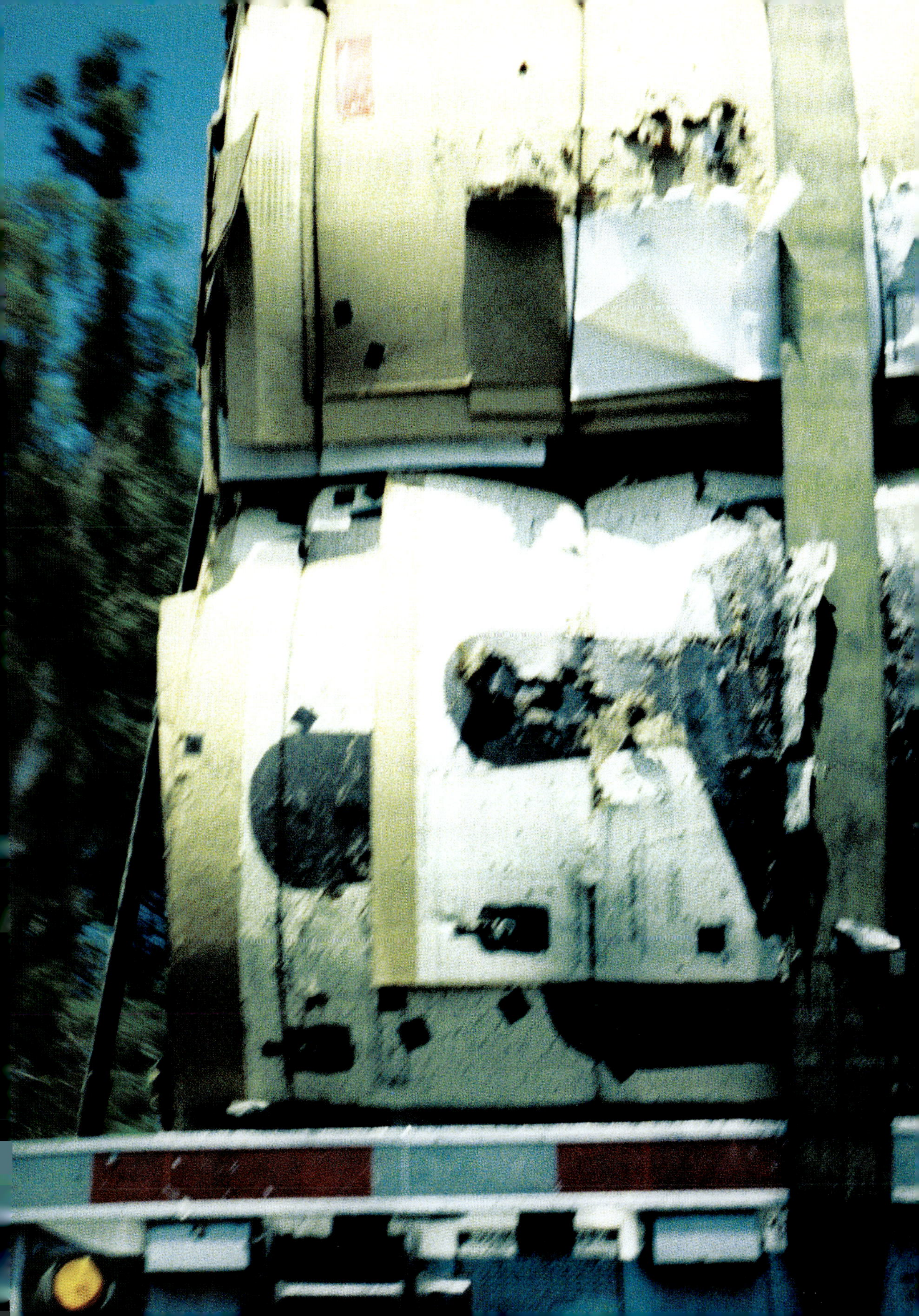

62

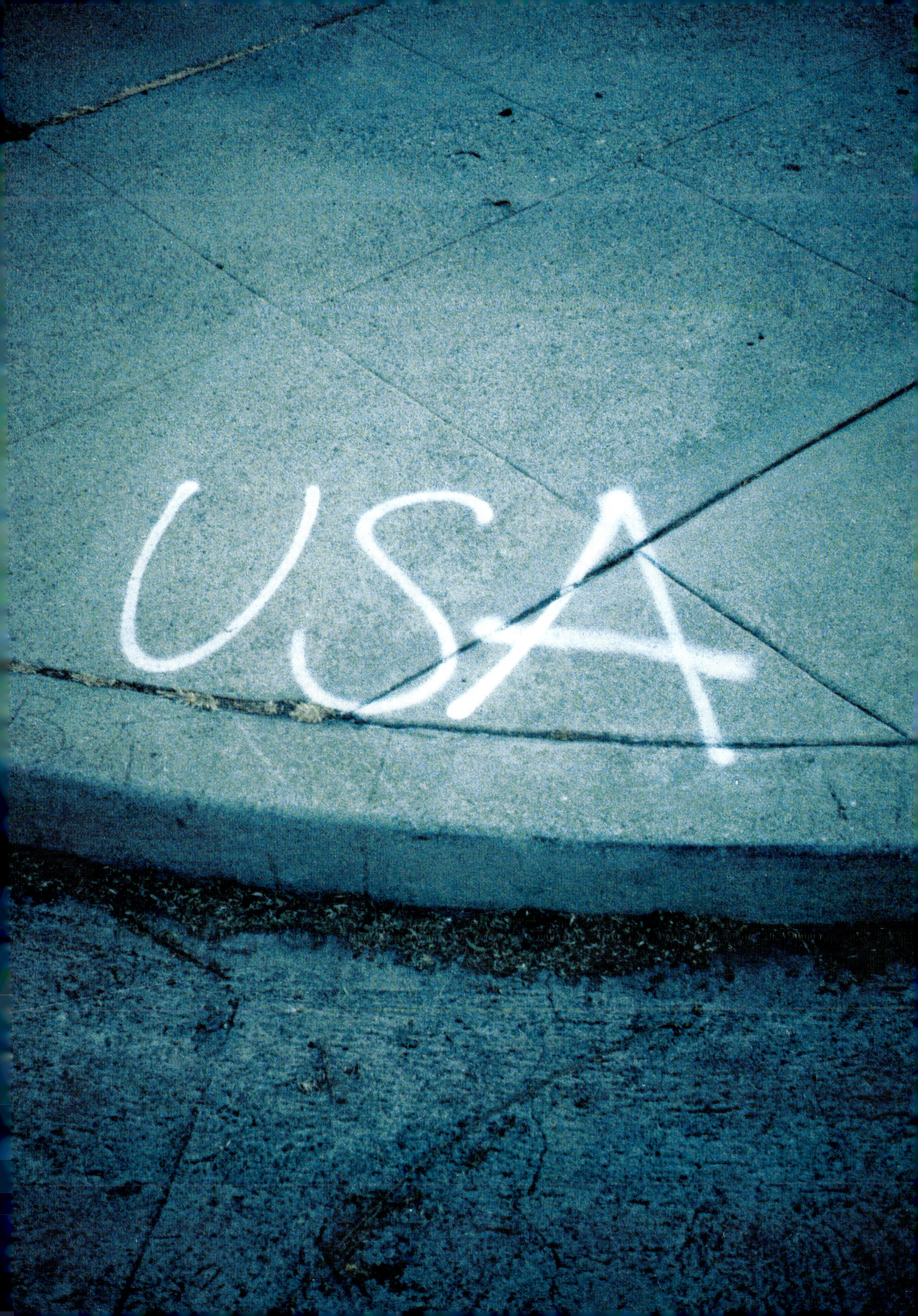
USA

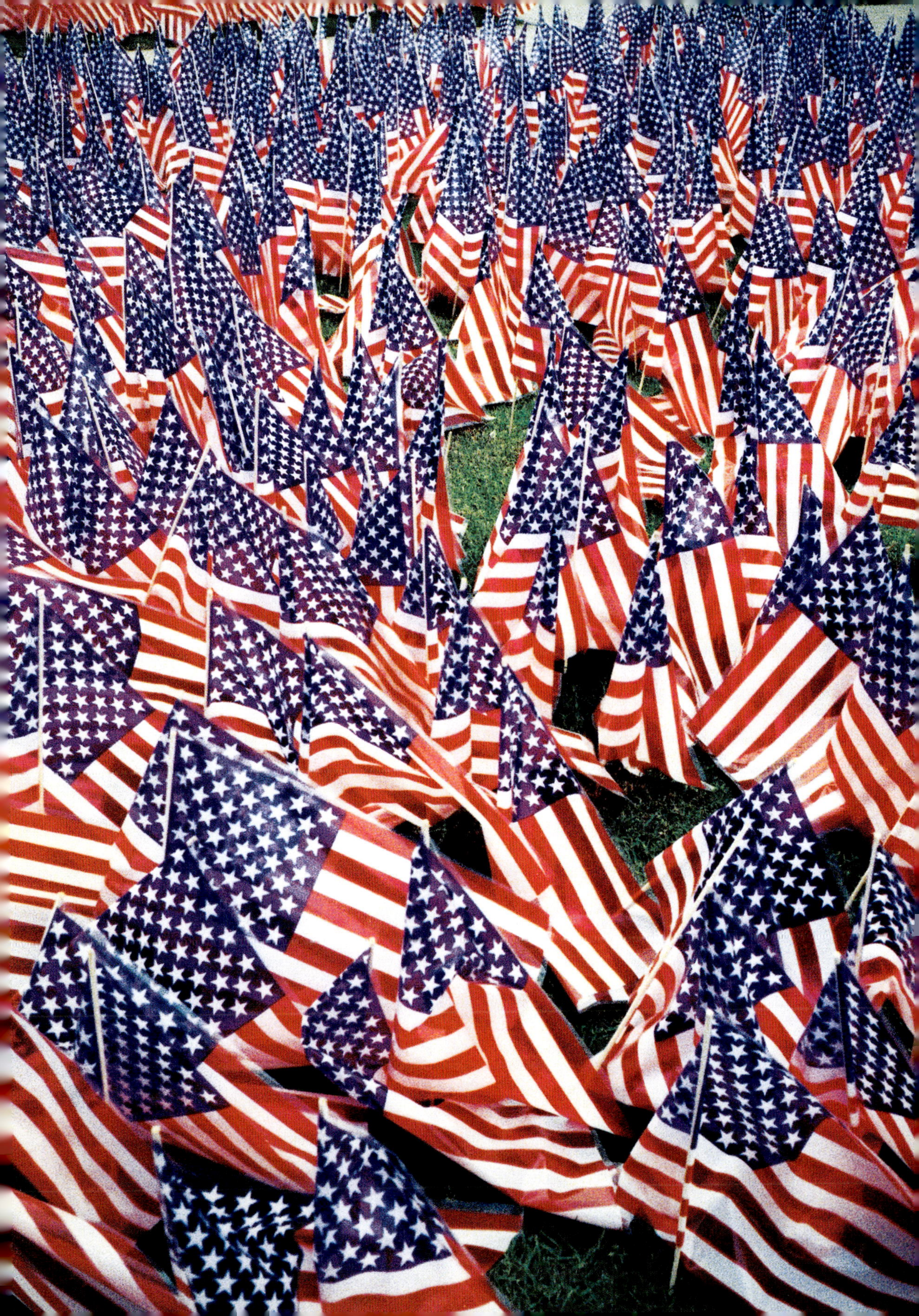

66

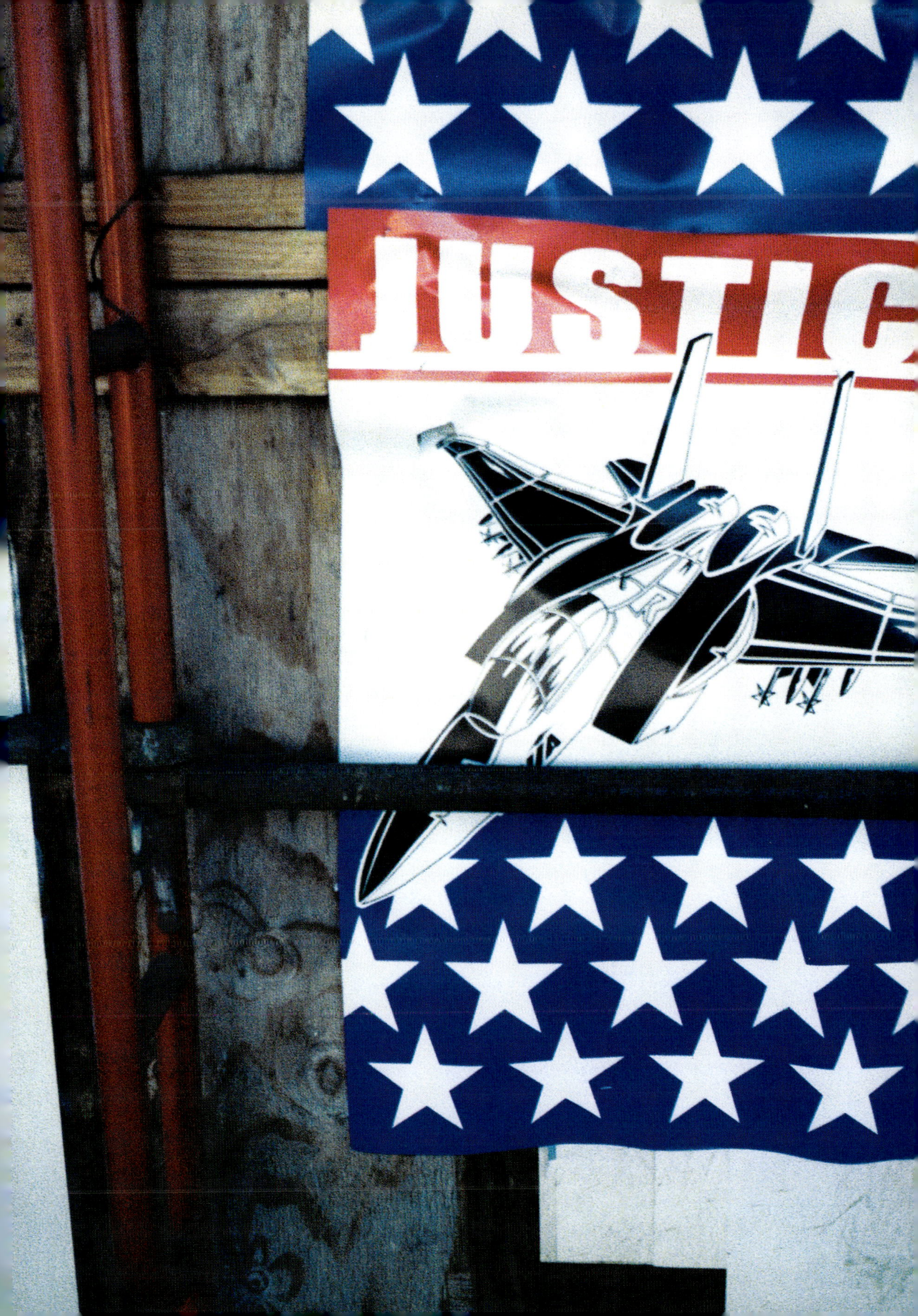
JUSTIC

68

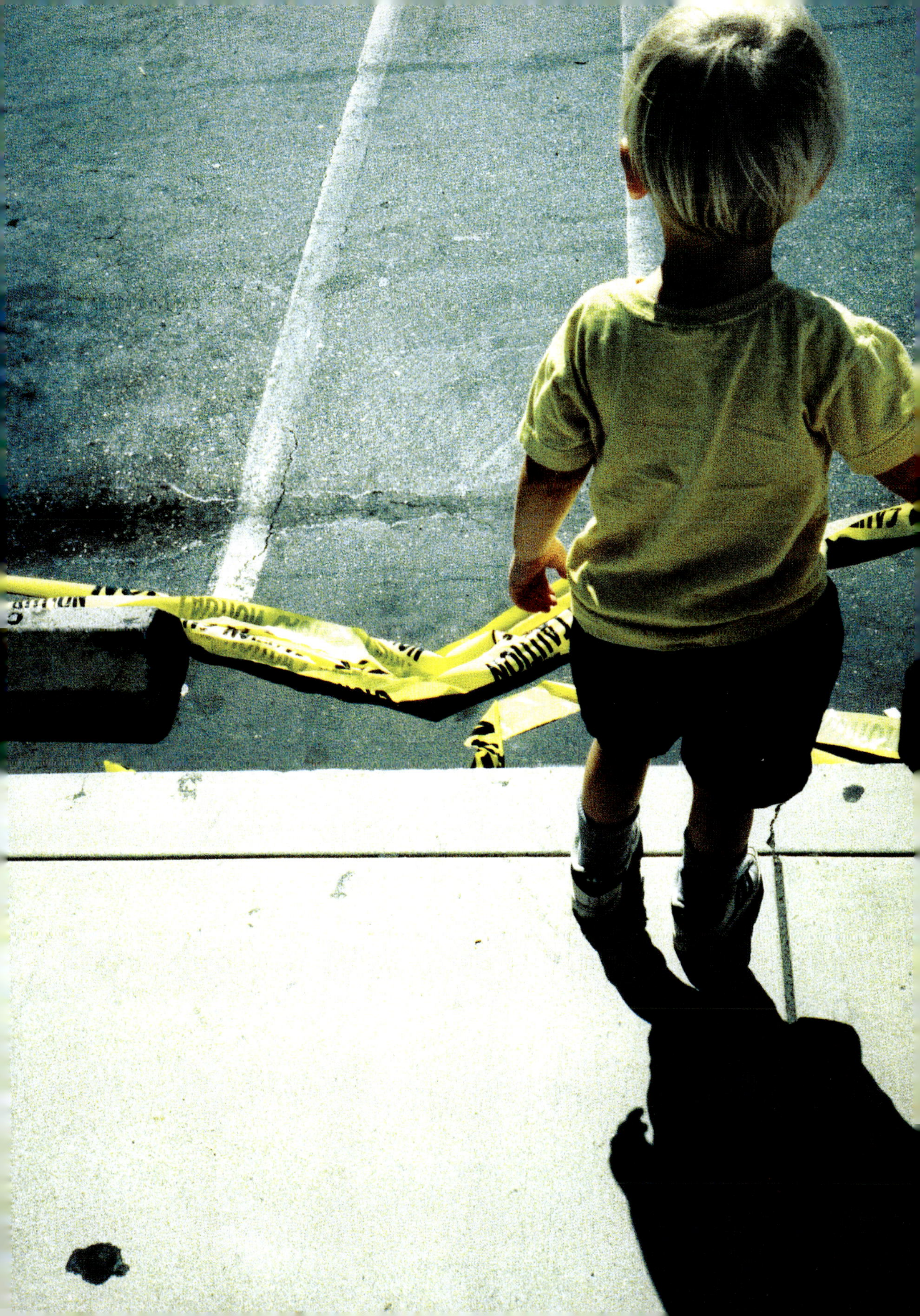

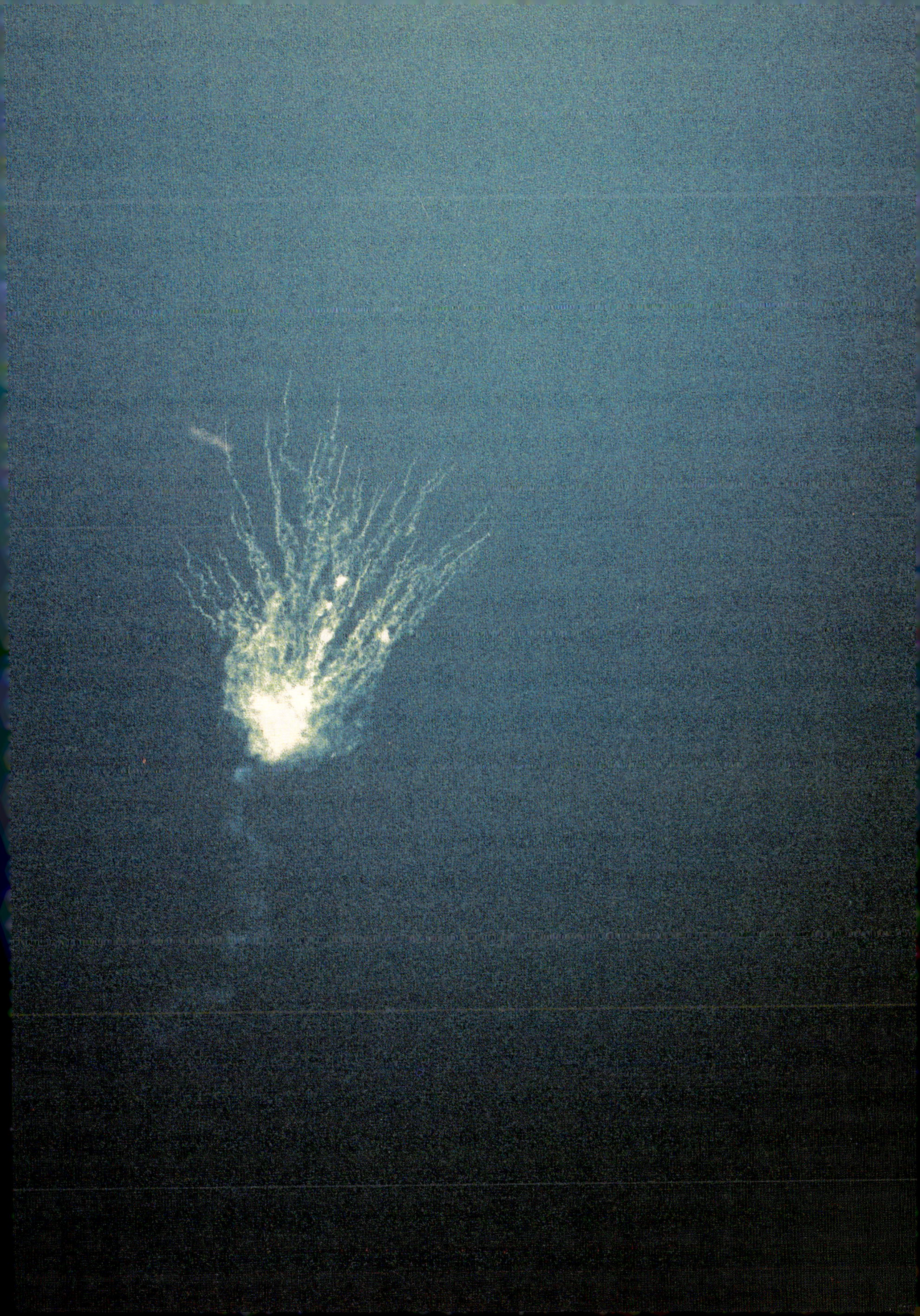

72

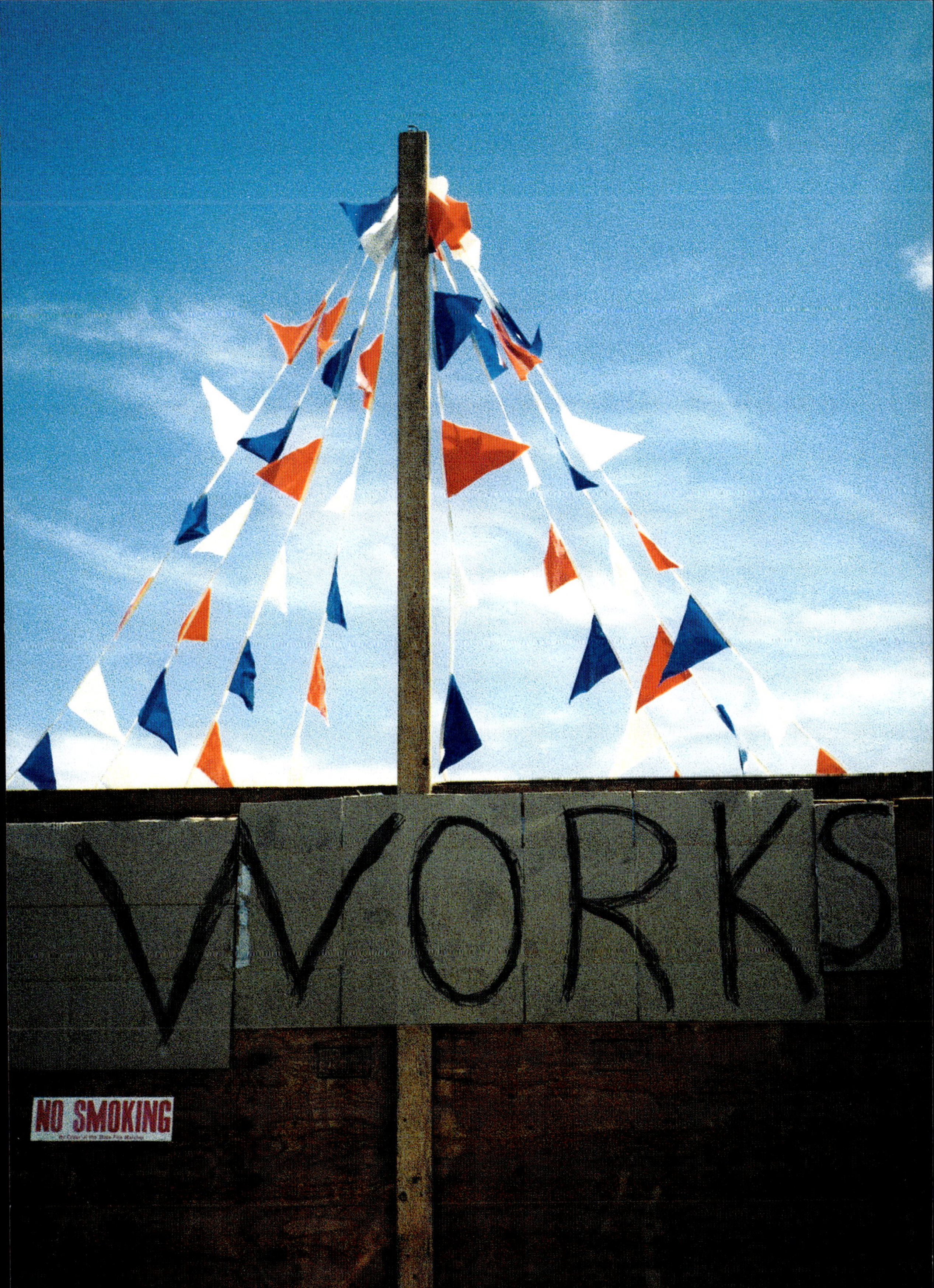
WORKS
NO SMOKING

74

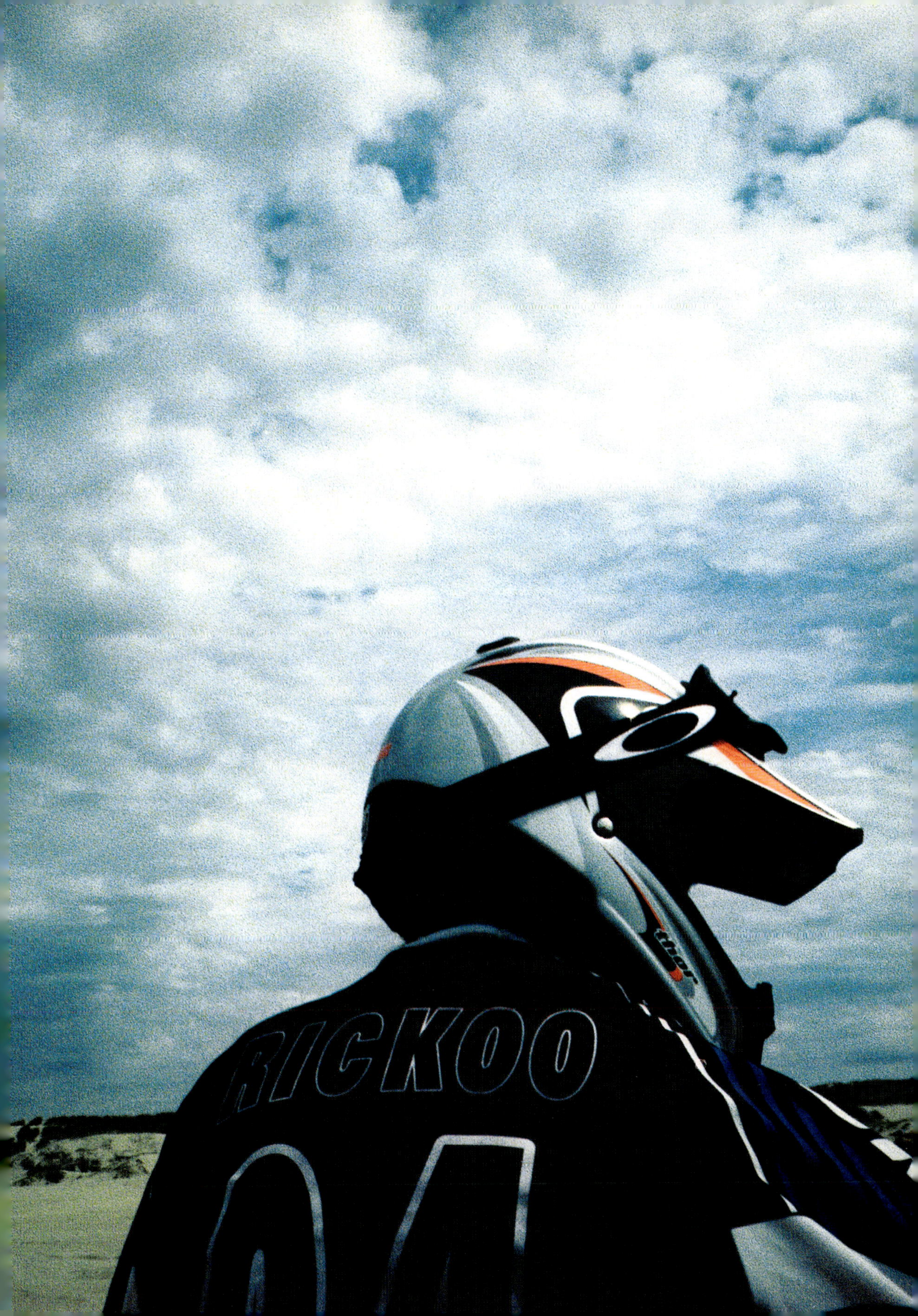
RICKOO

76

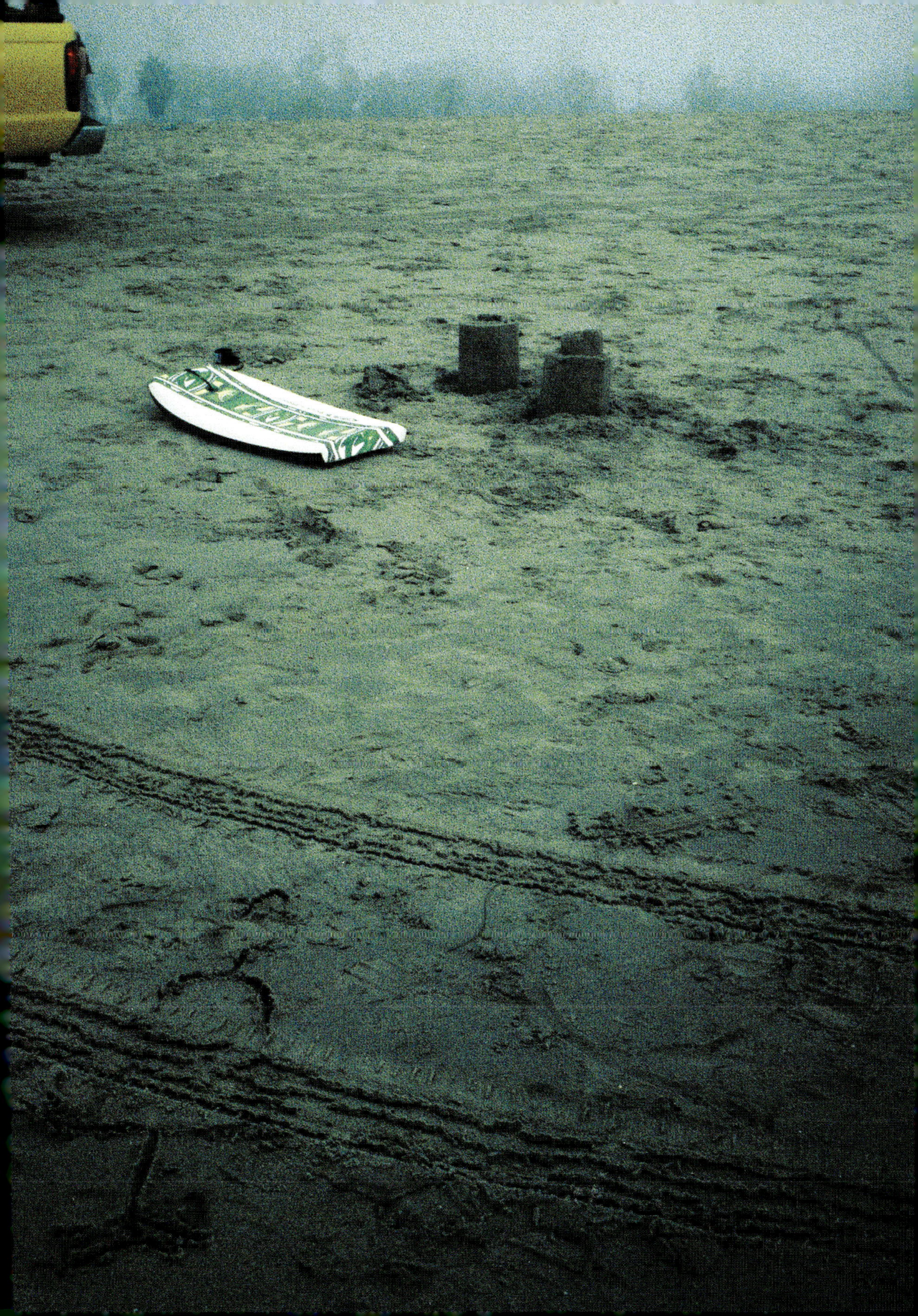

78

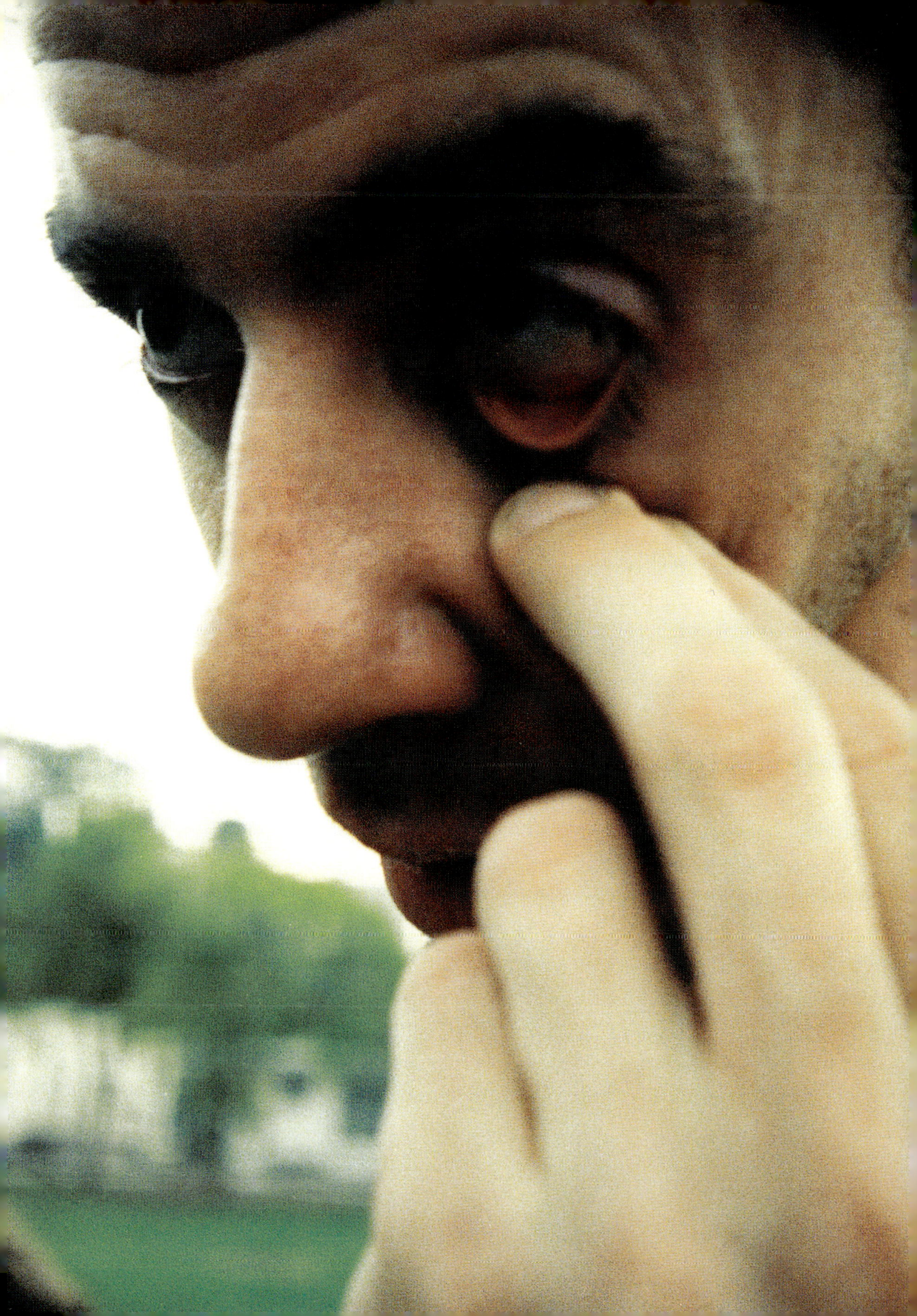

80

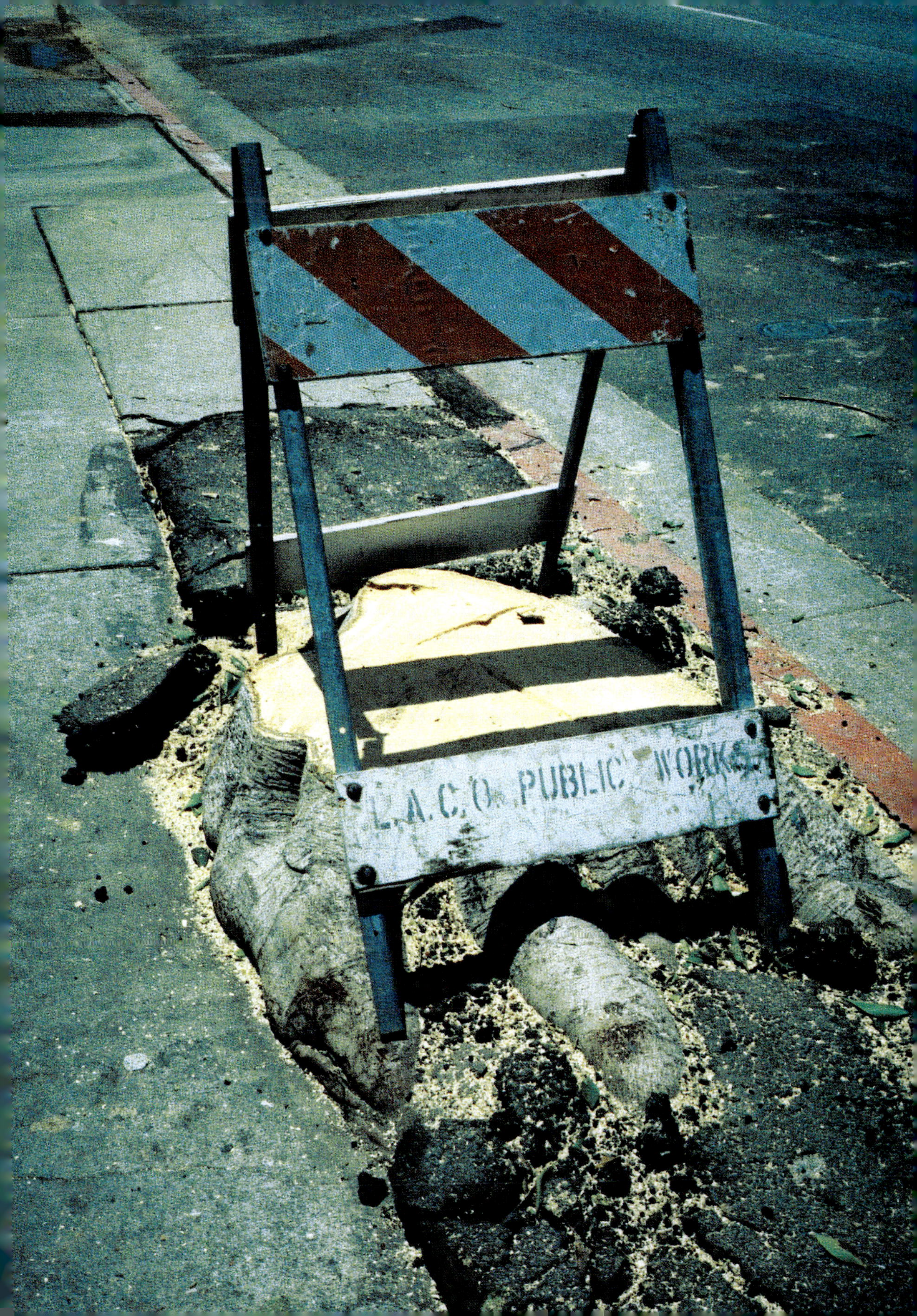
L.A.C.O. PUBLIC WORKS

82

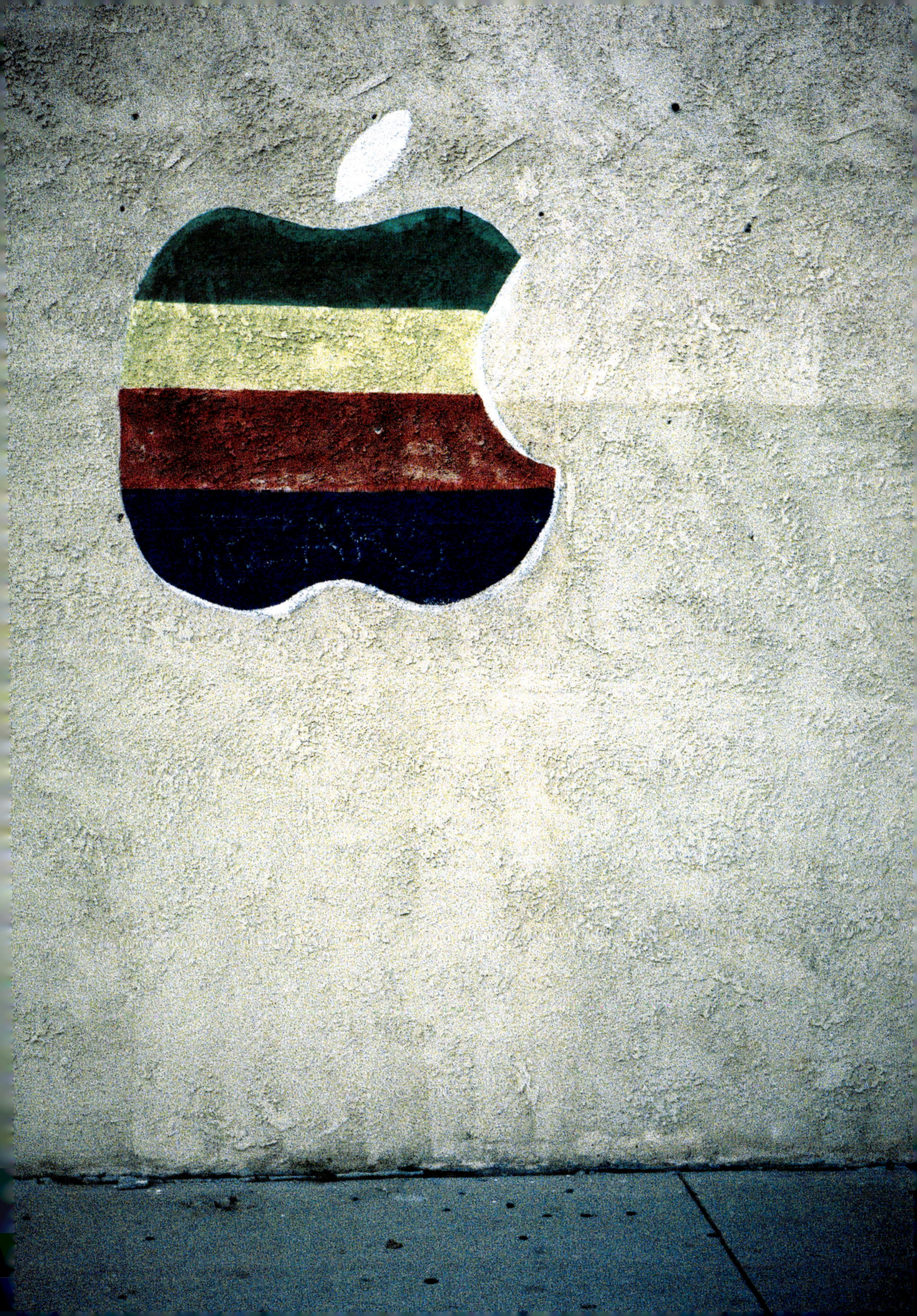

84

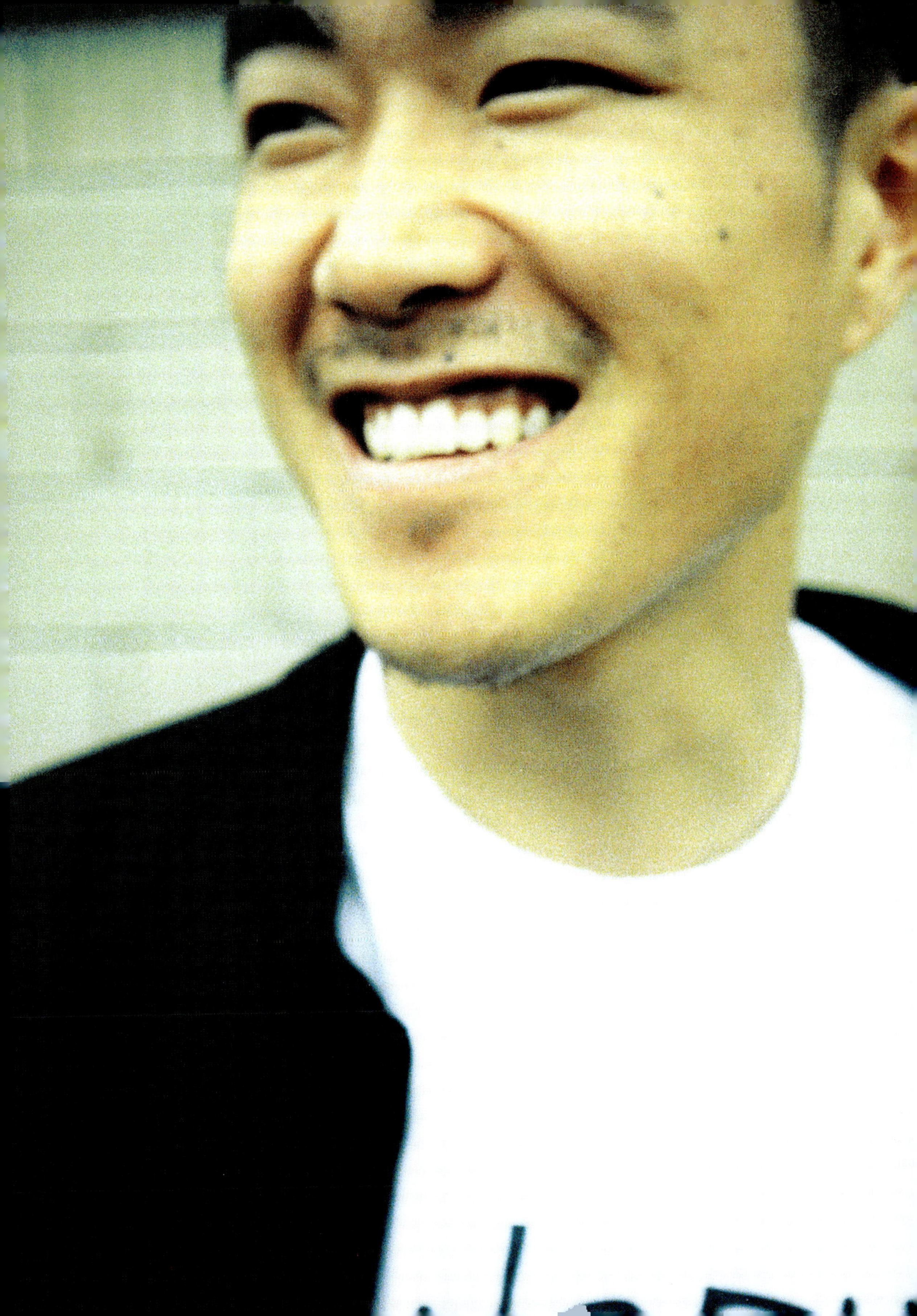

86

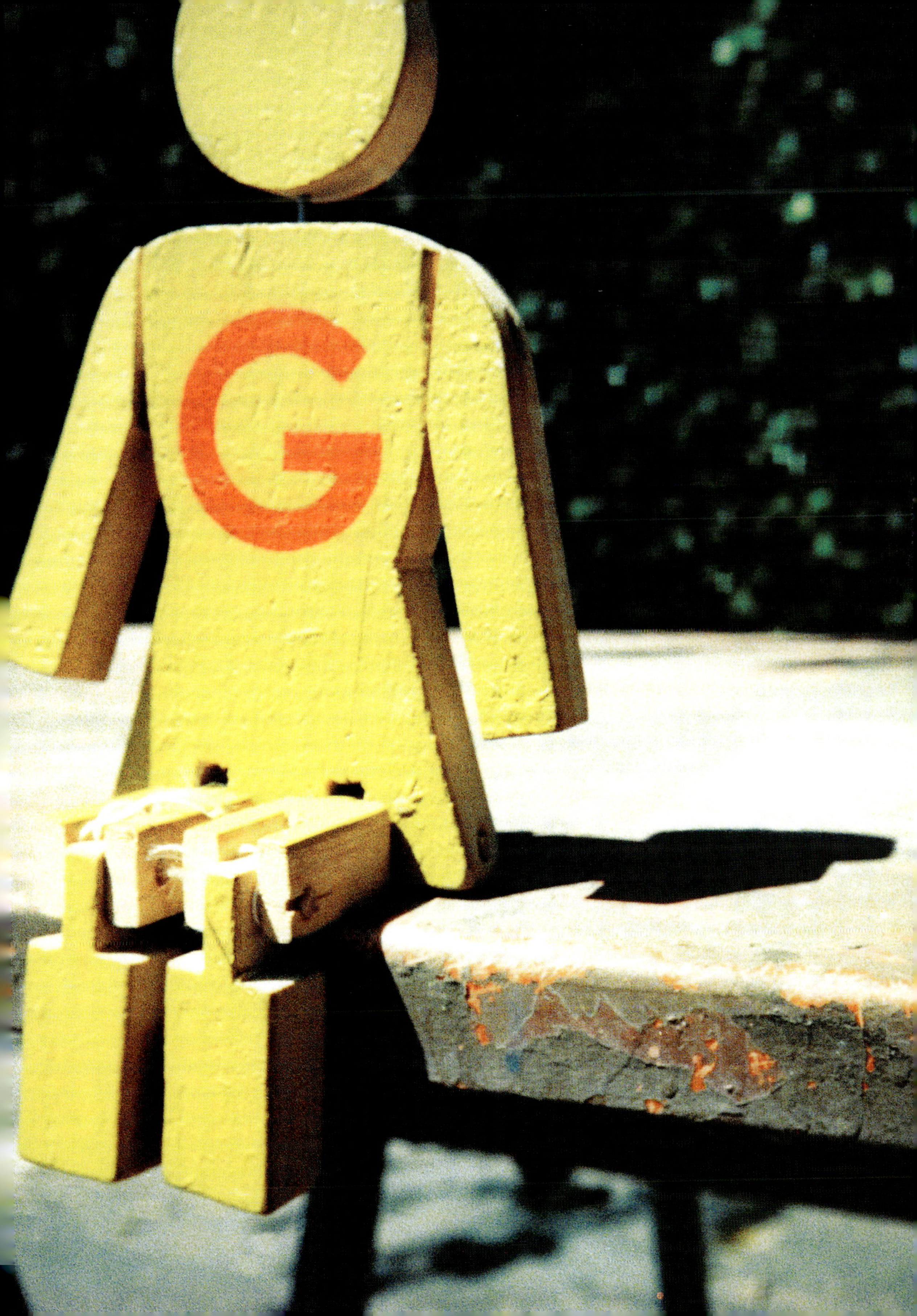
G

88

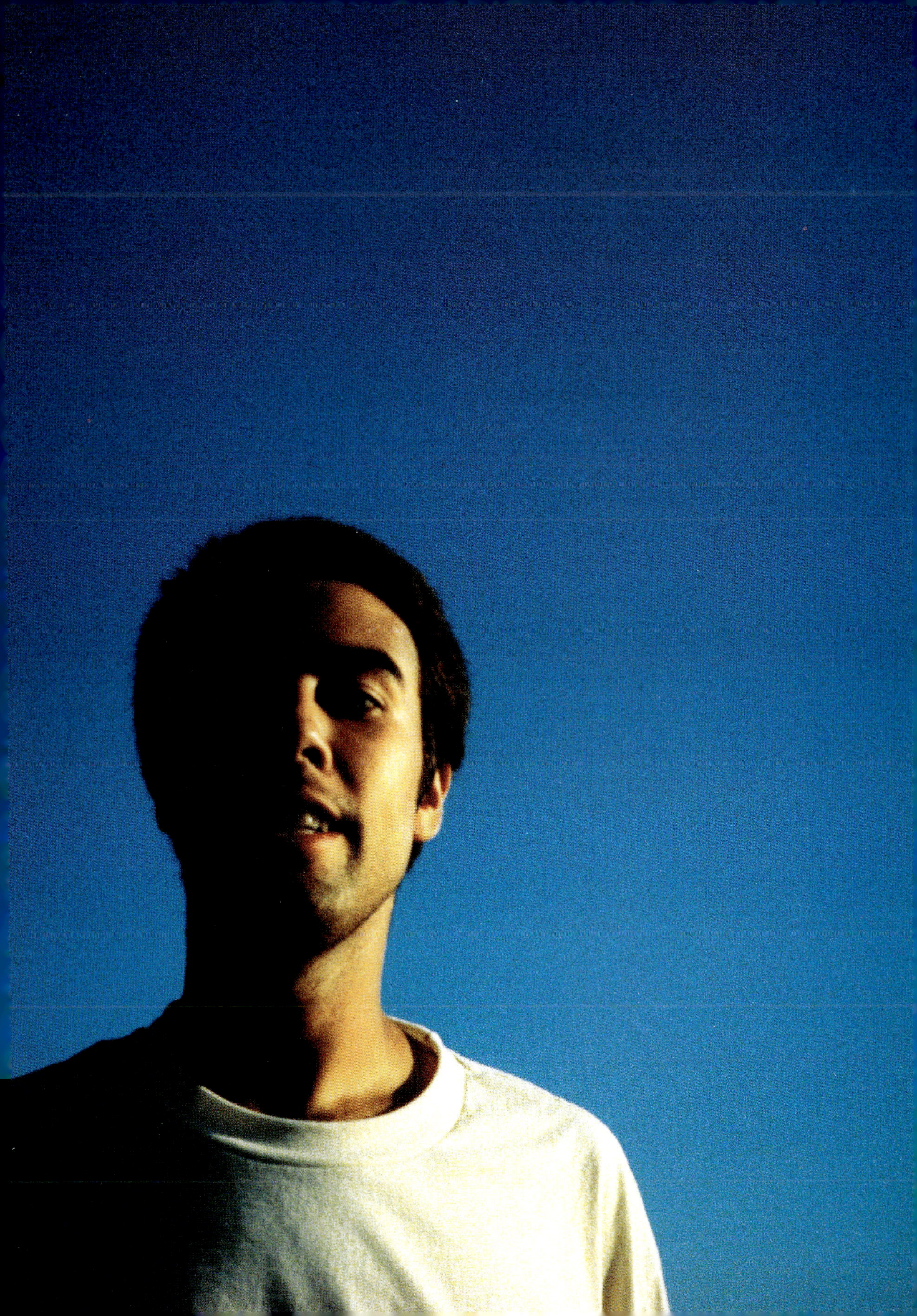

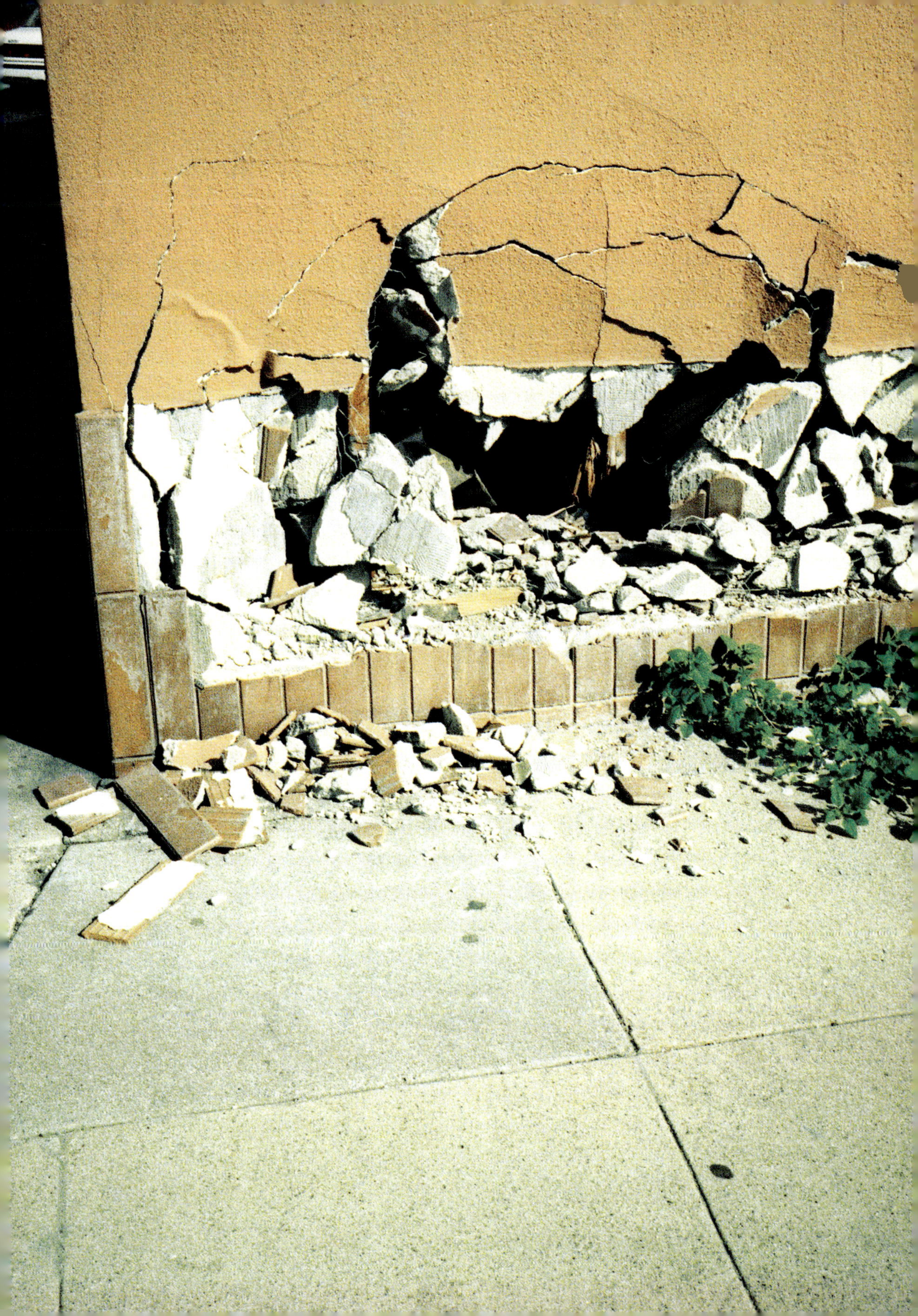

92

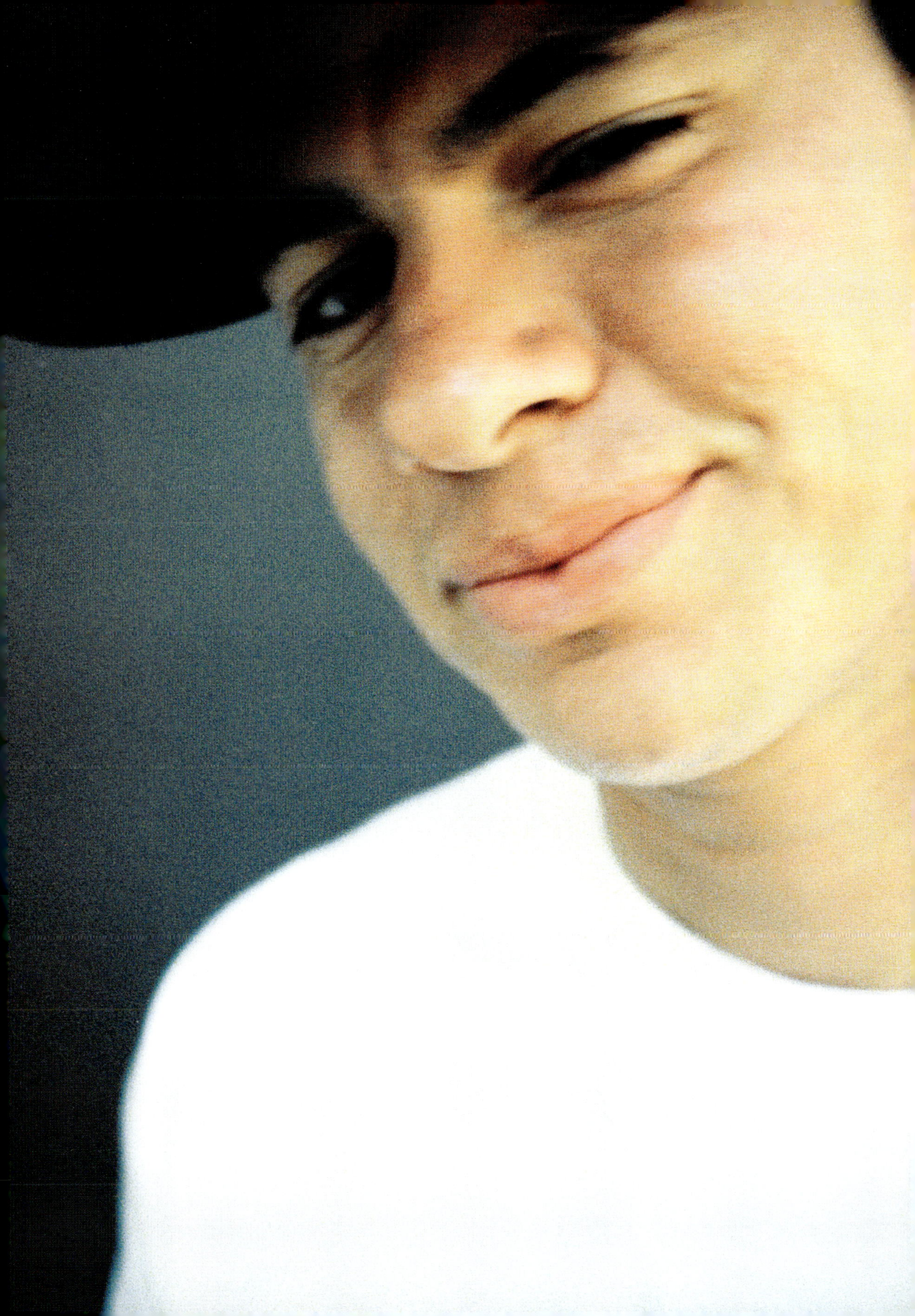

94

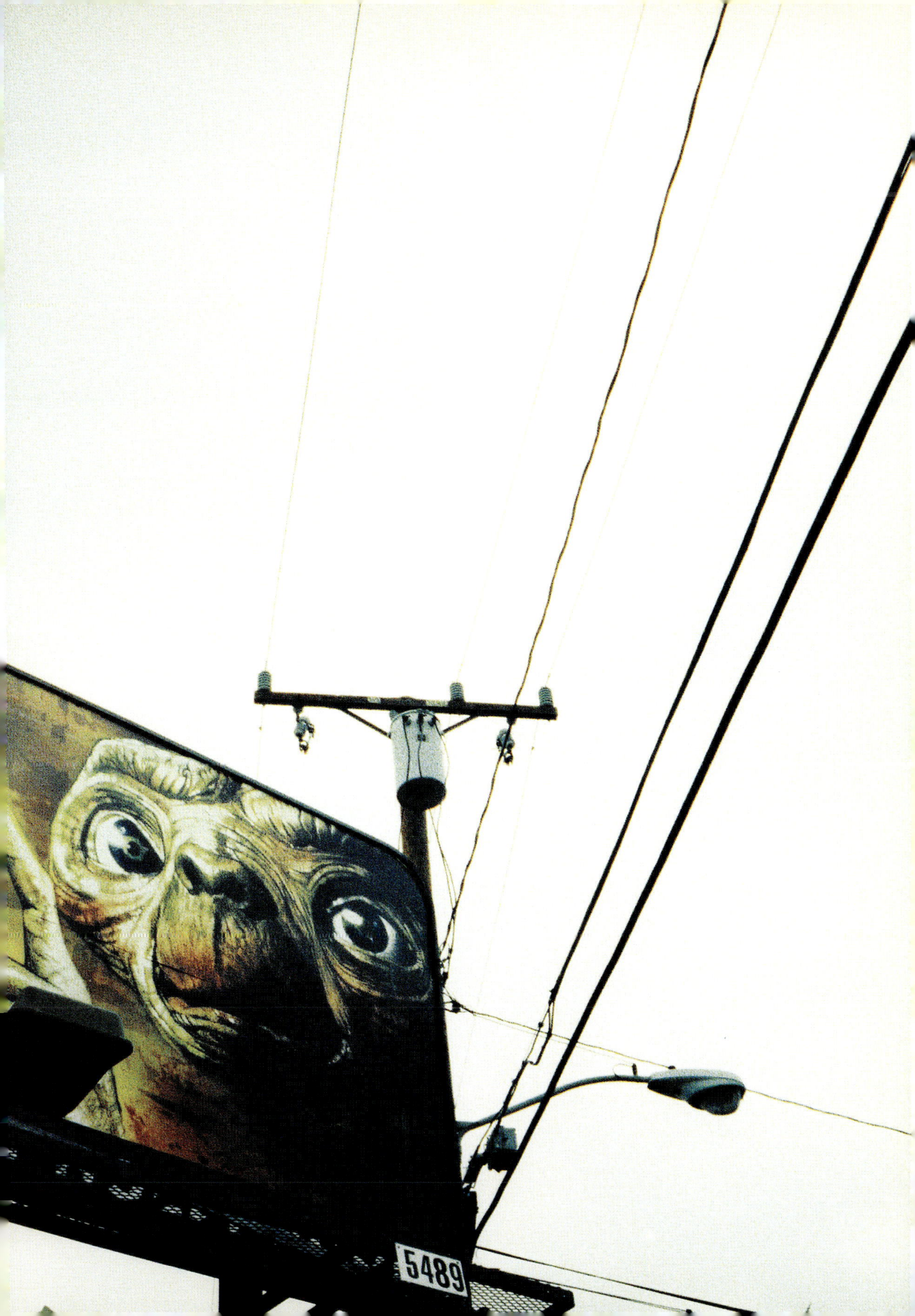
5489

96

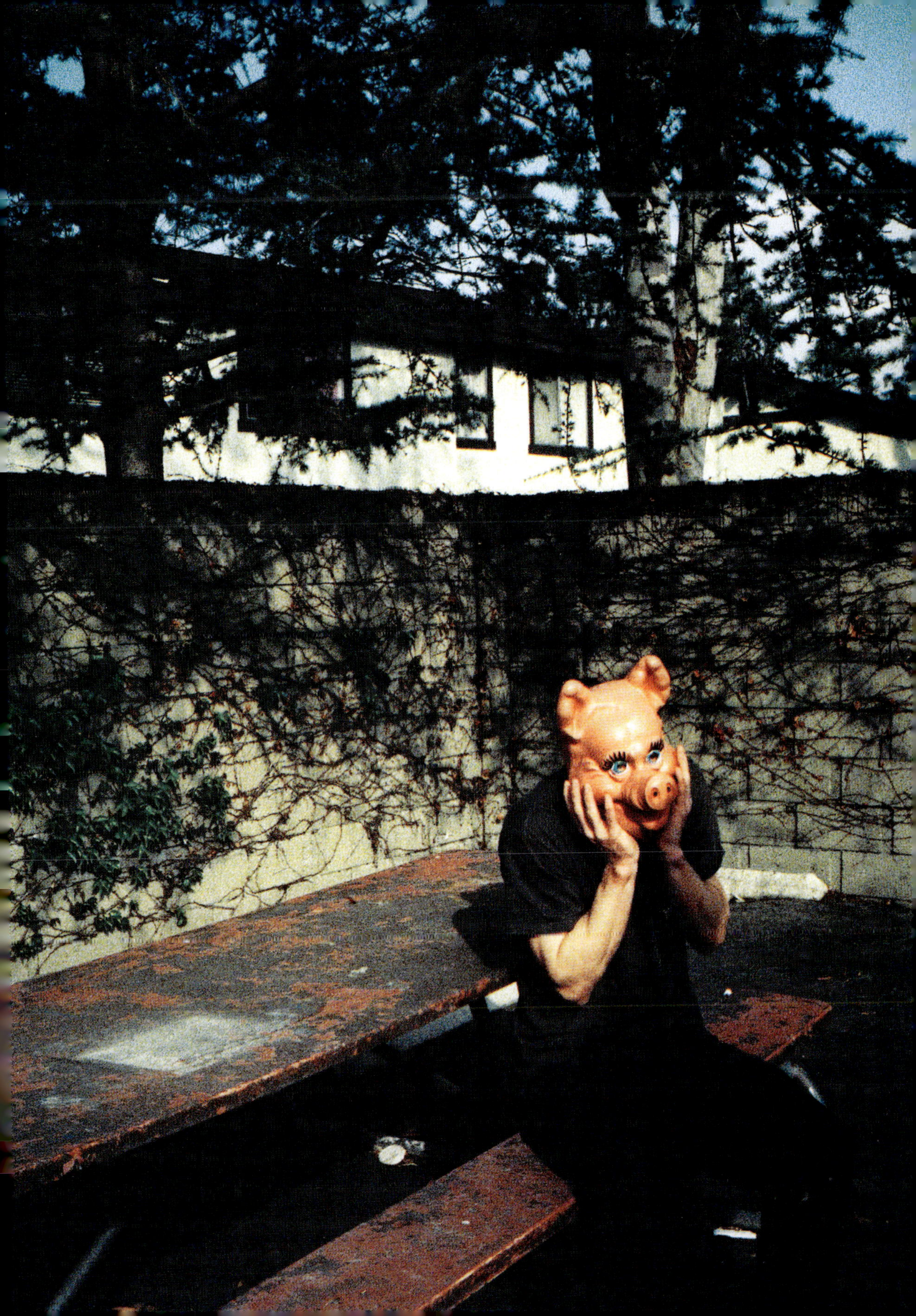

98

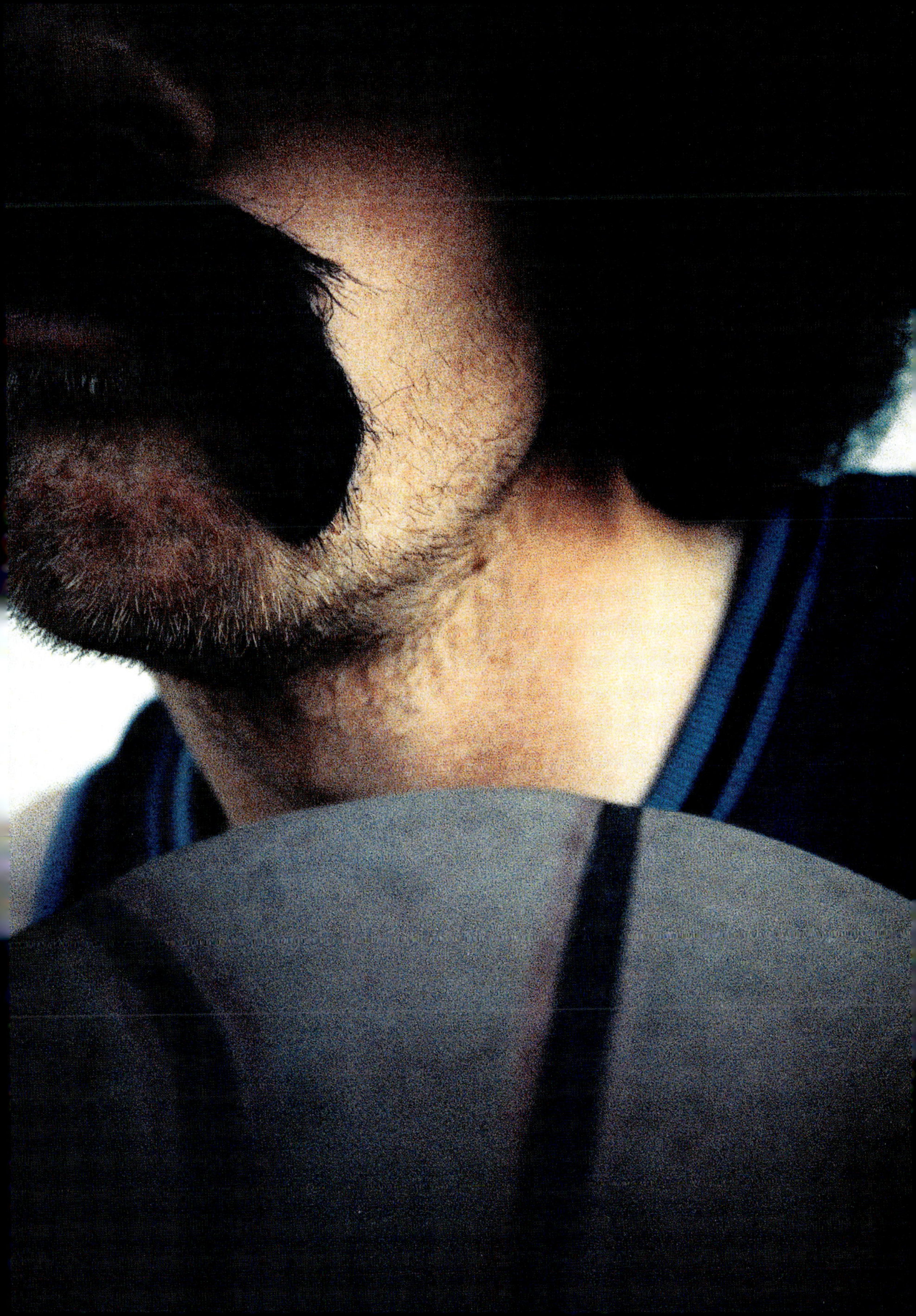

100

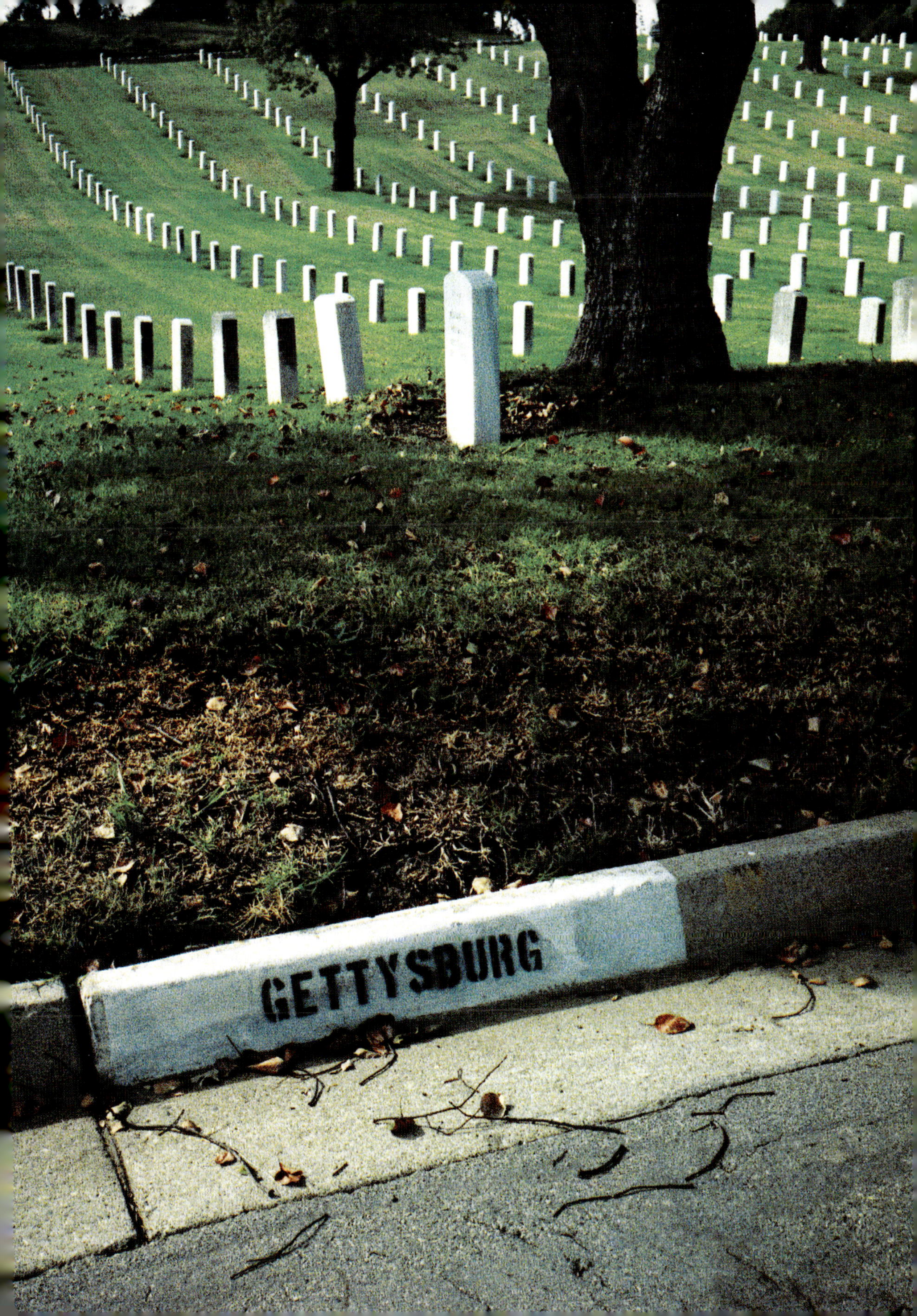
GETTYSBURG

102

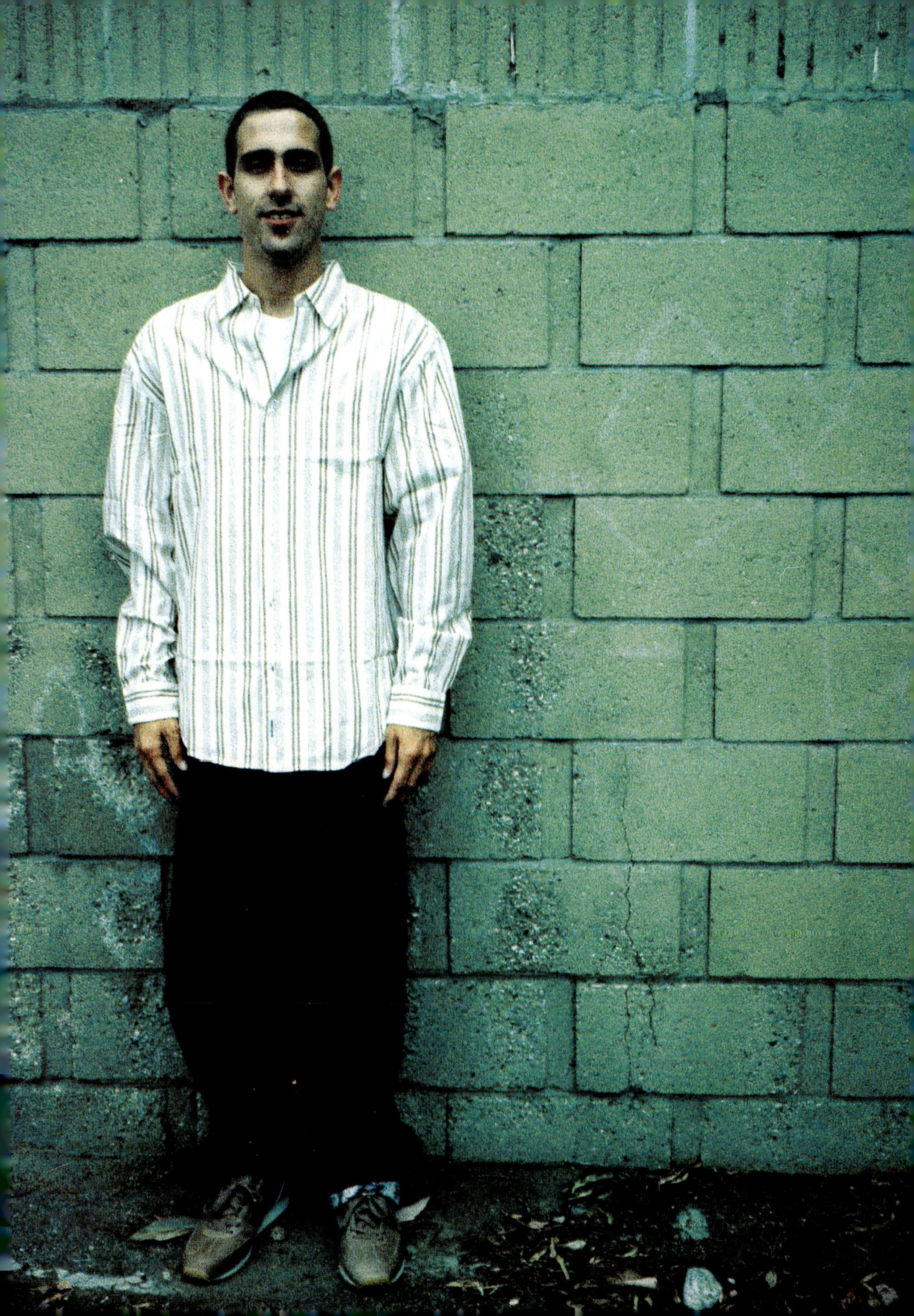

104

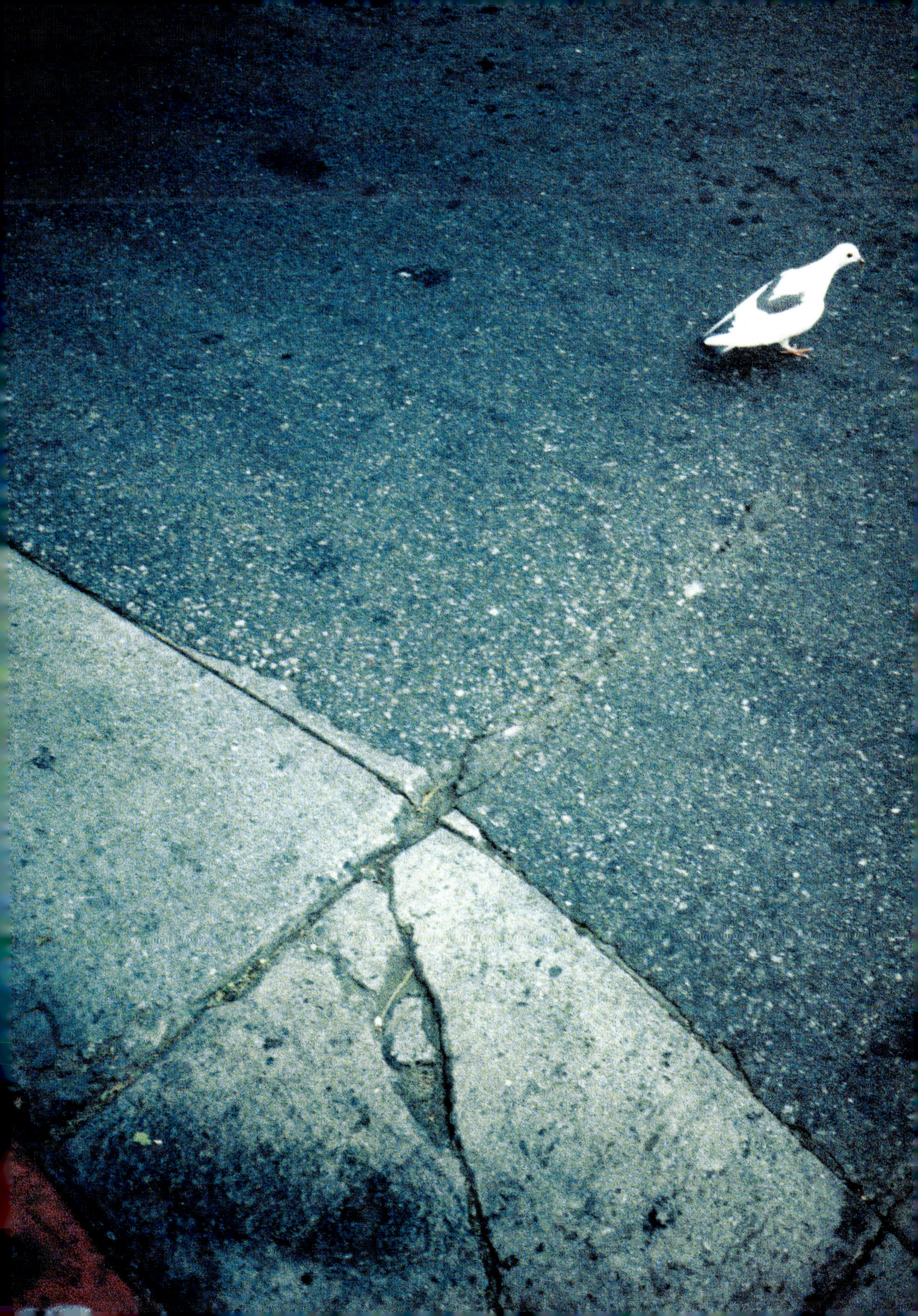

106

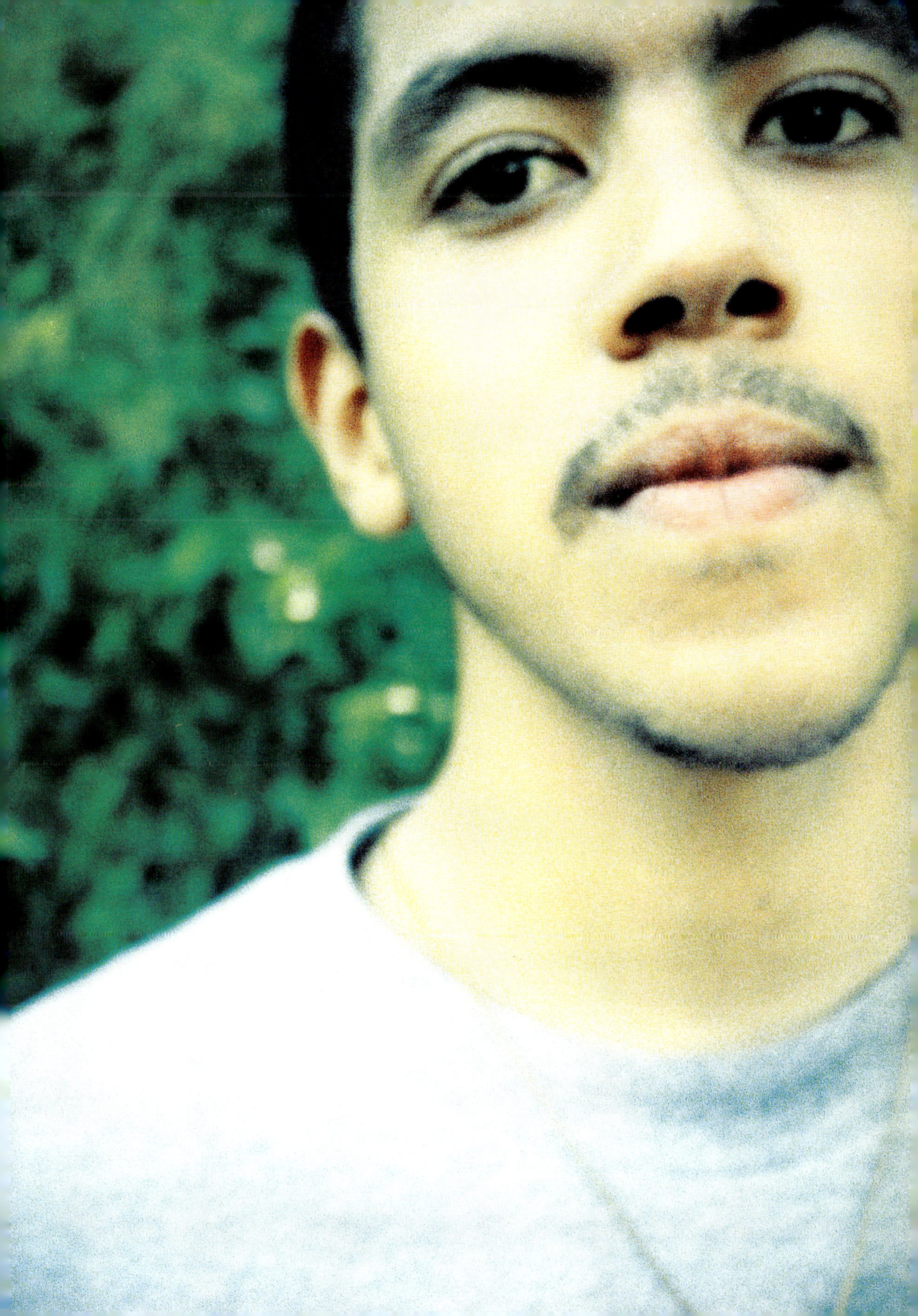

108

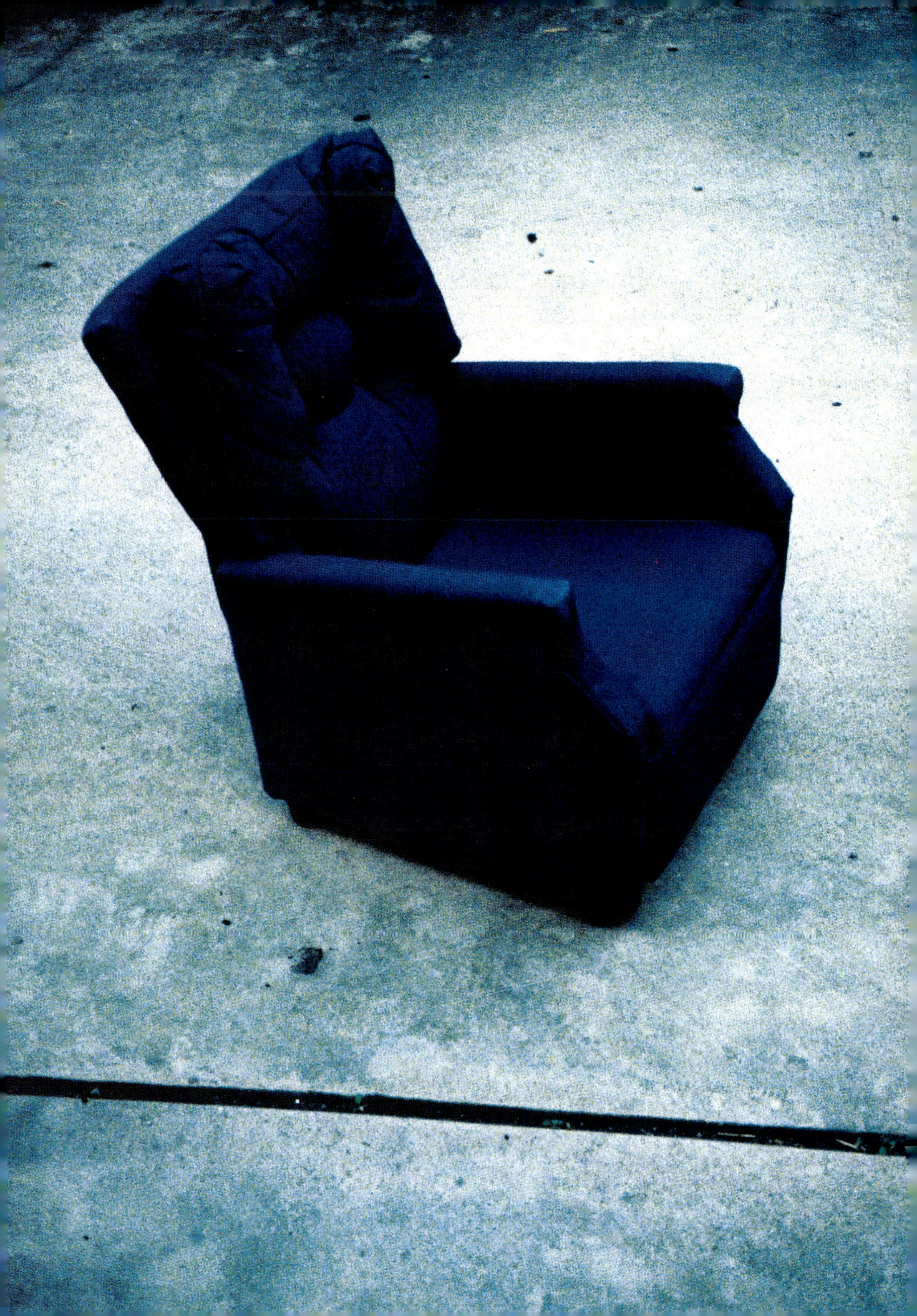

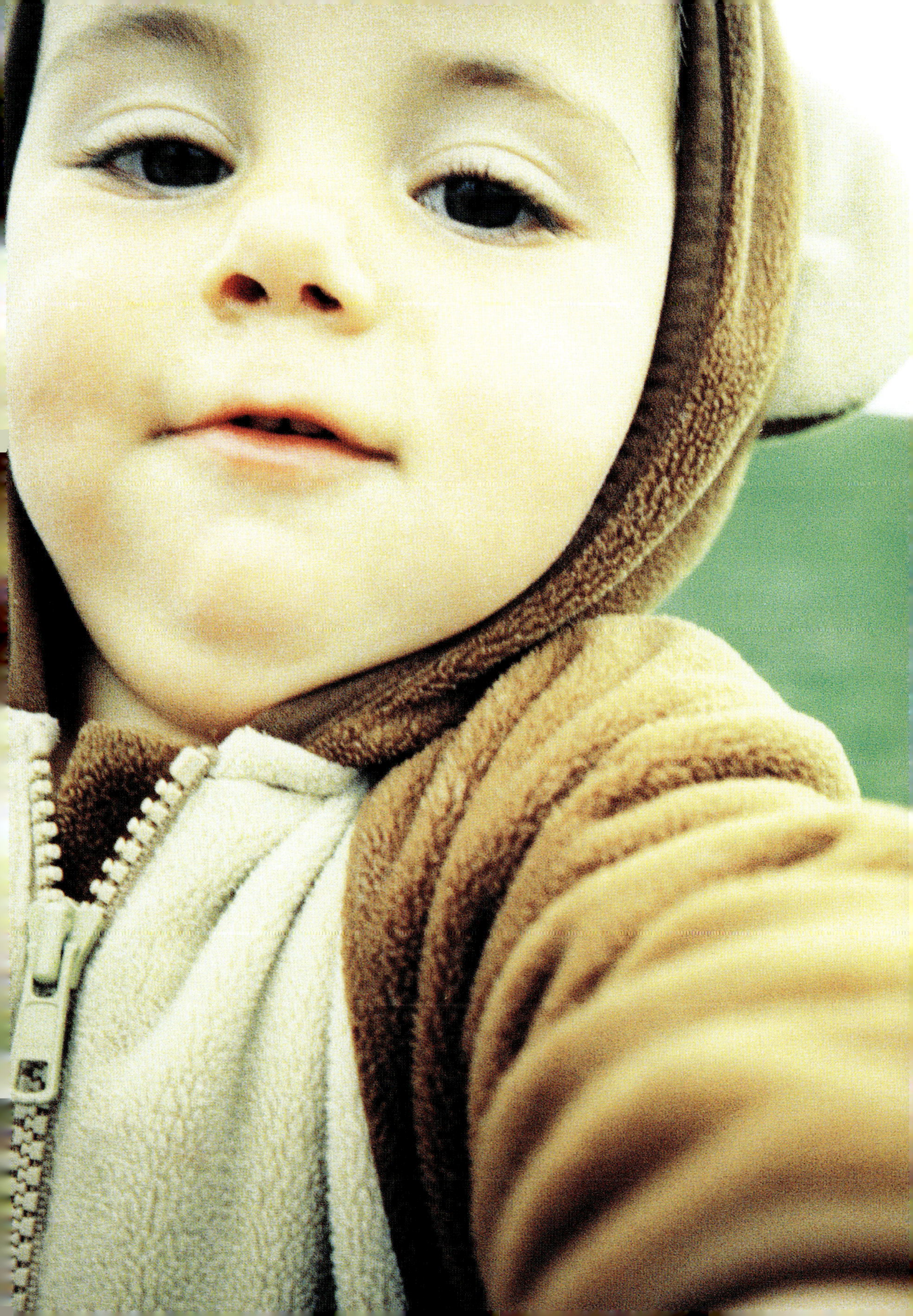

112

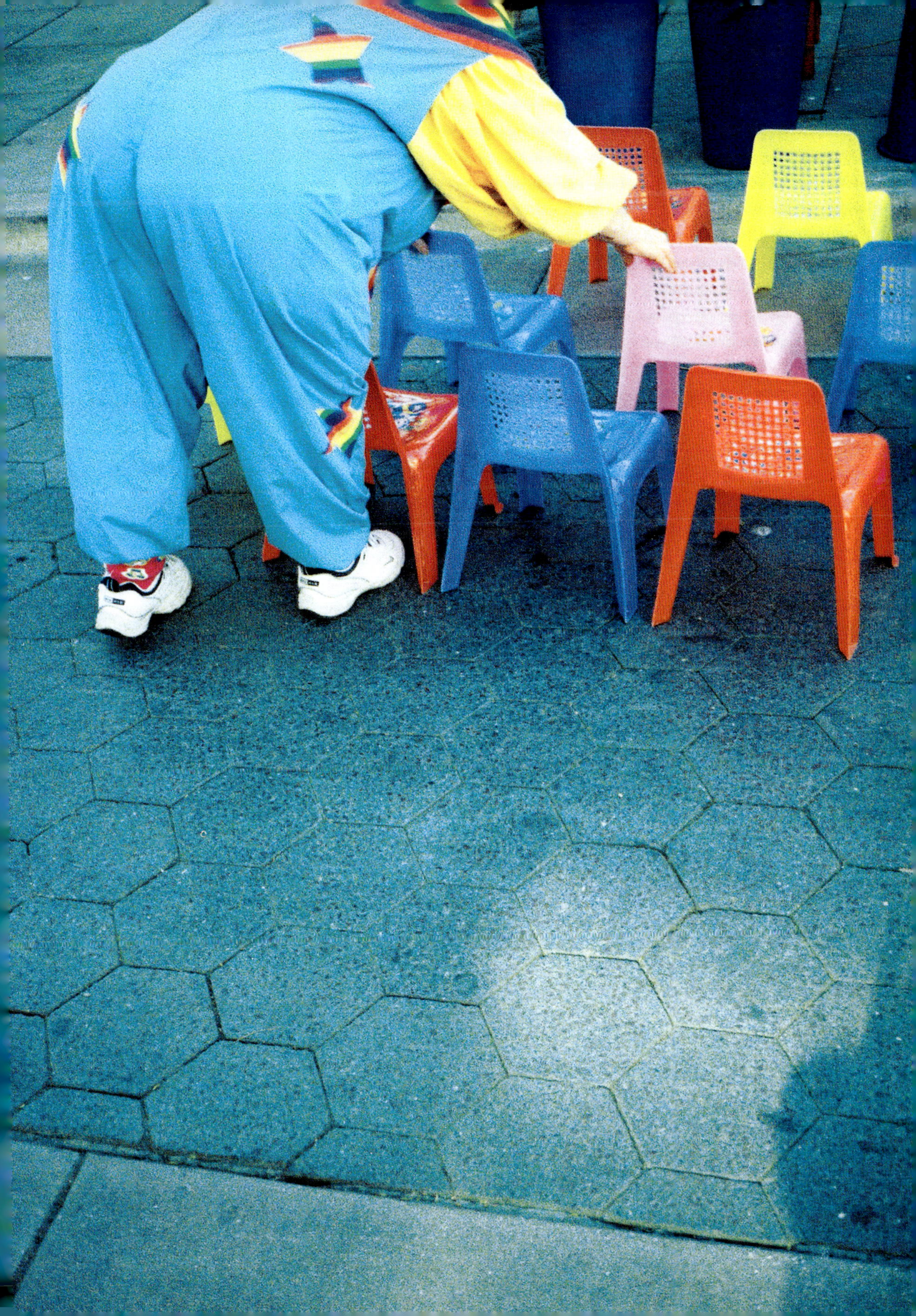

114

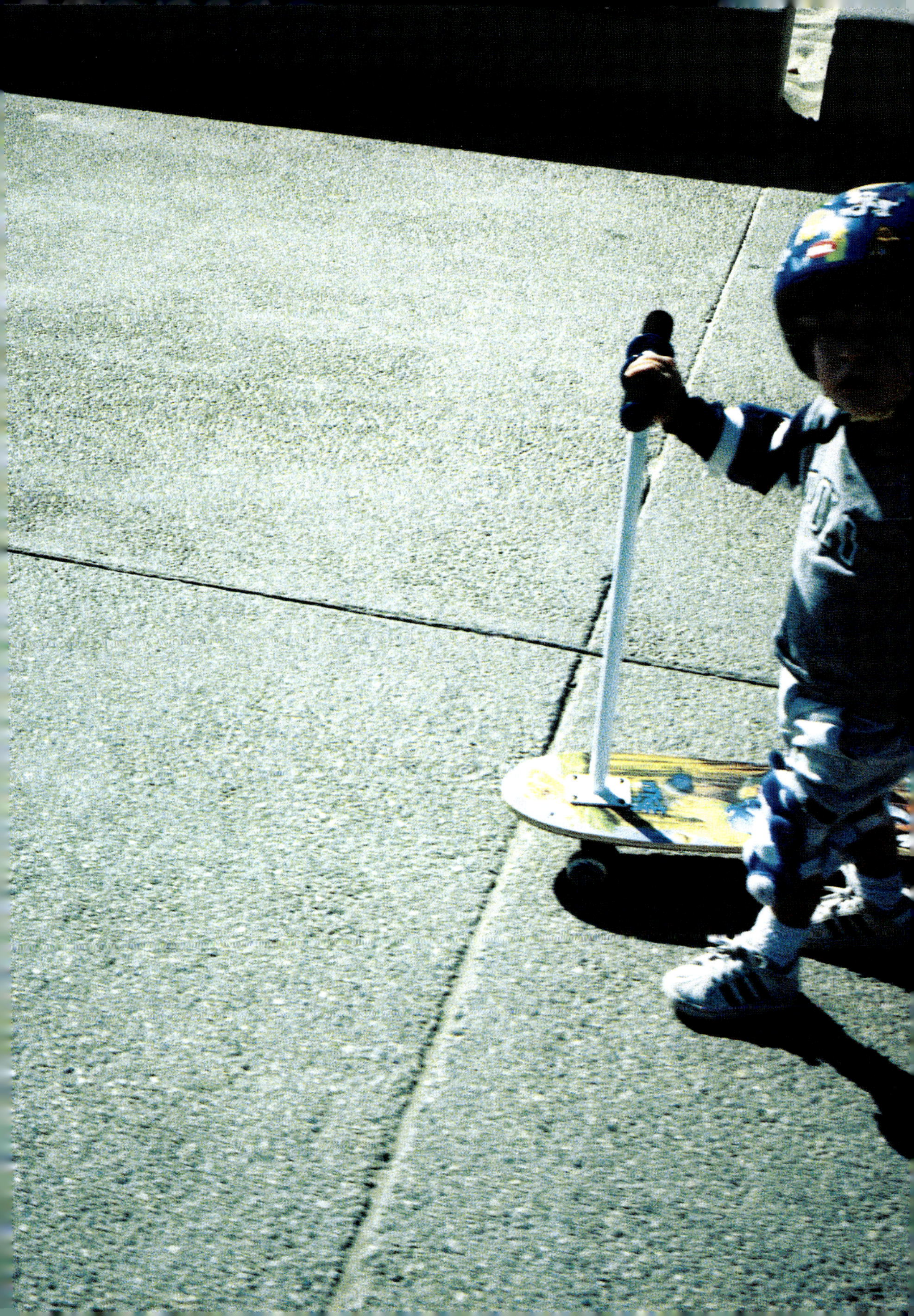

116

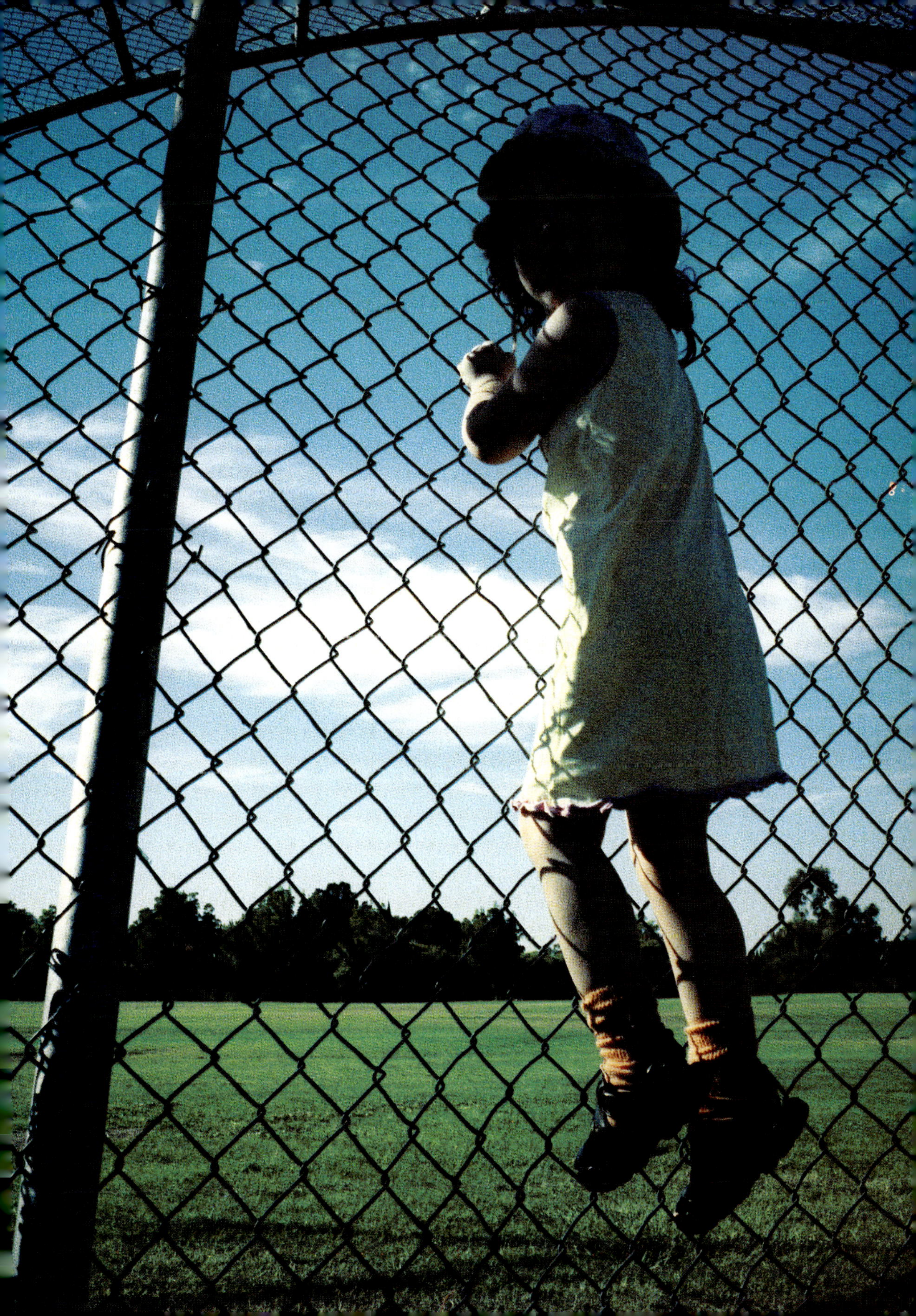

118

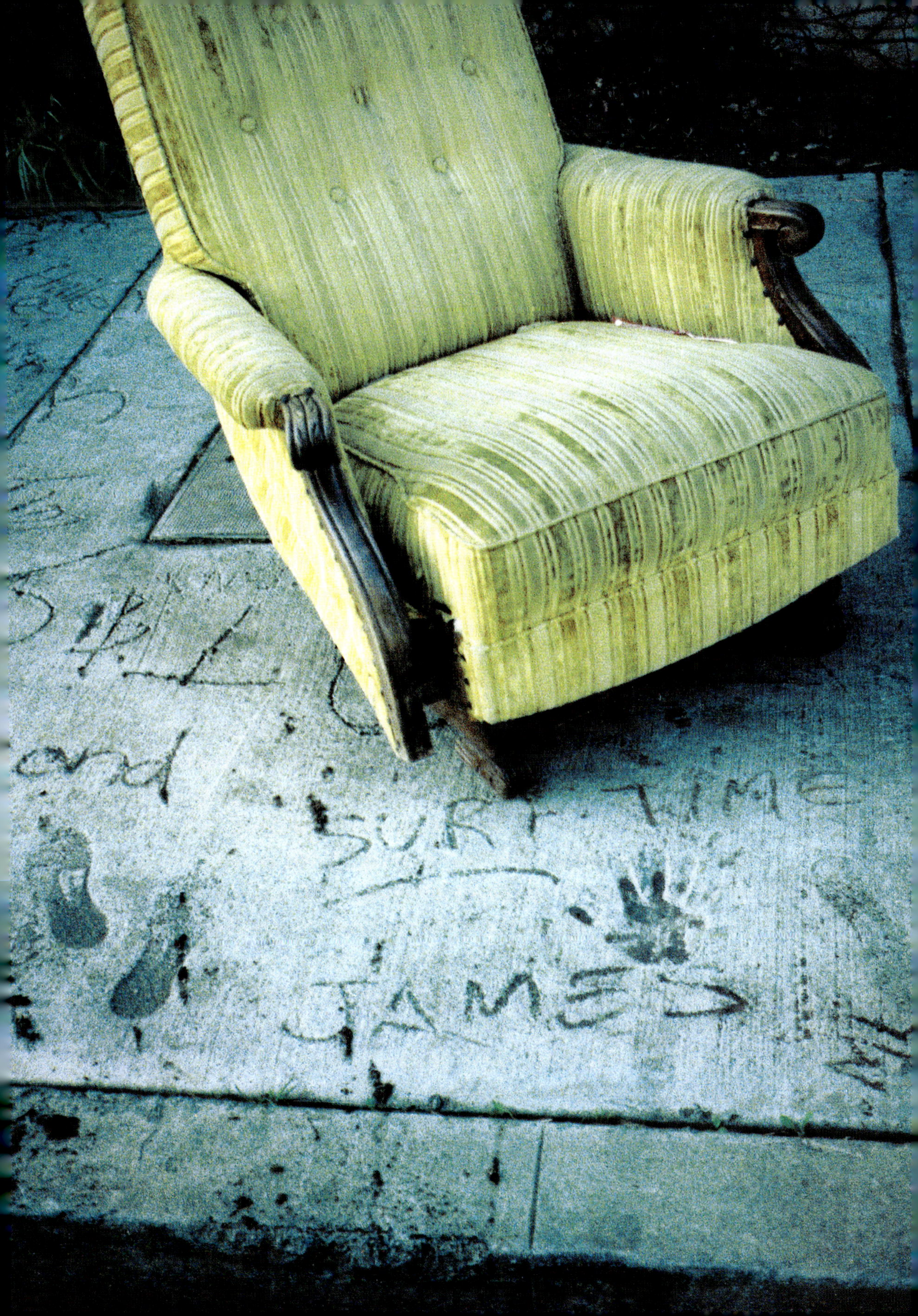
and
SURF TIME
JAMES

120

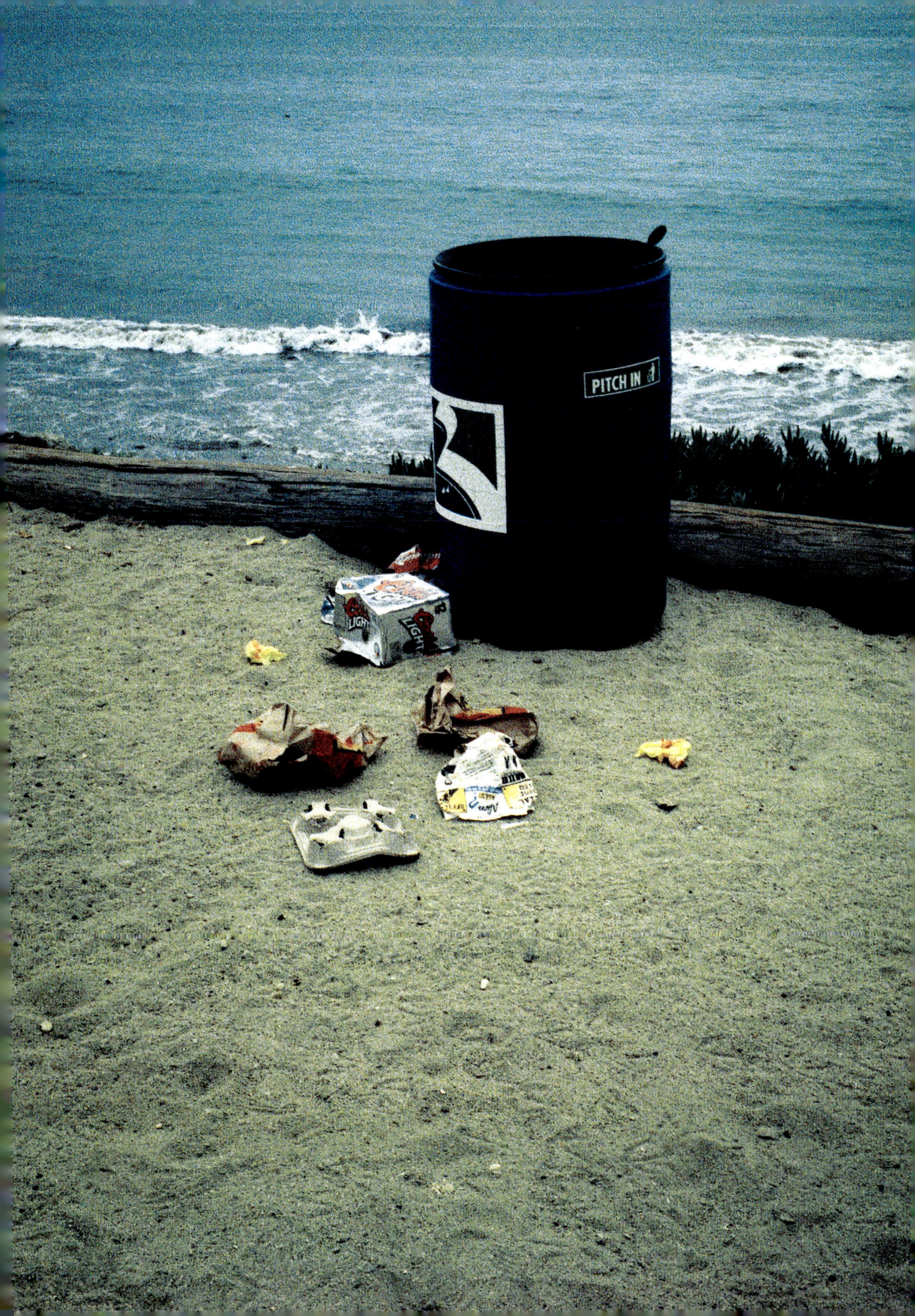
PITCH IN

122

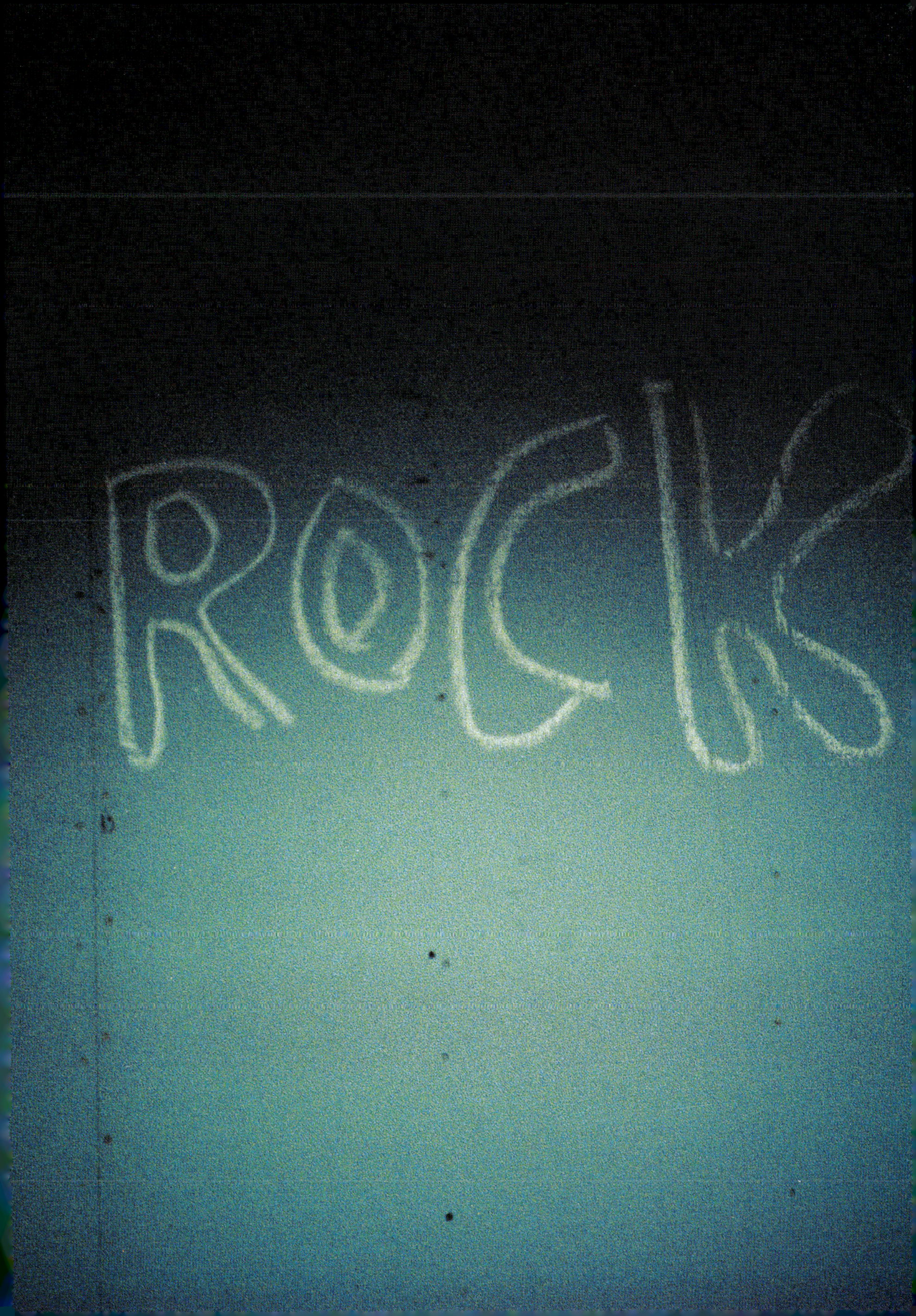
ROCK

124

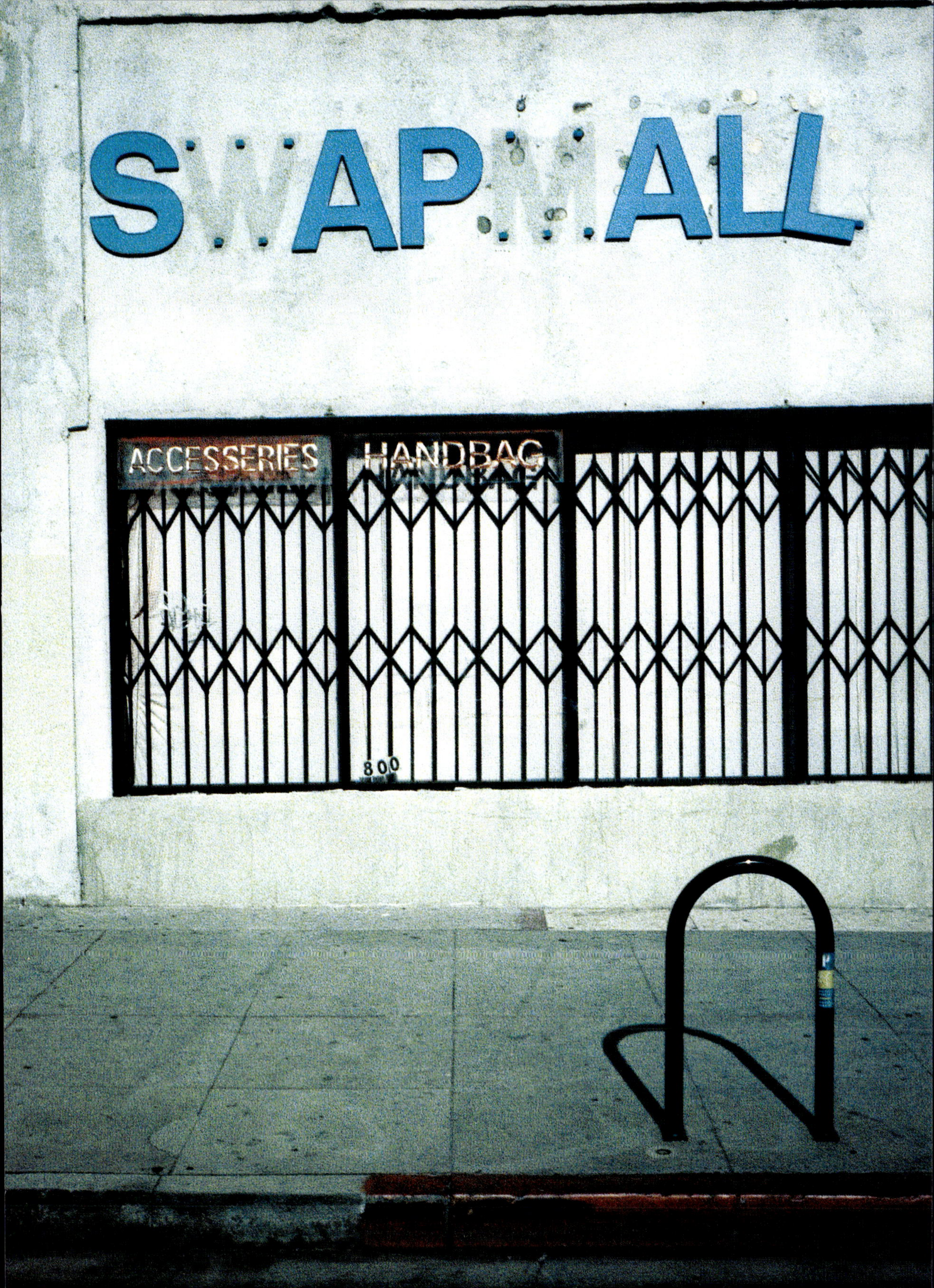
S AP ALL
ACCESSERIES
HANDBAG
800

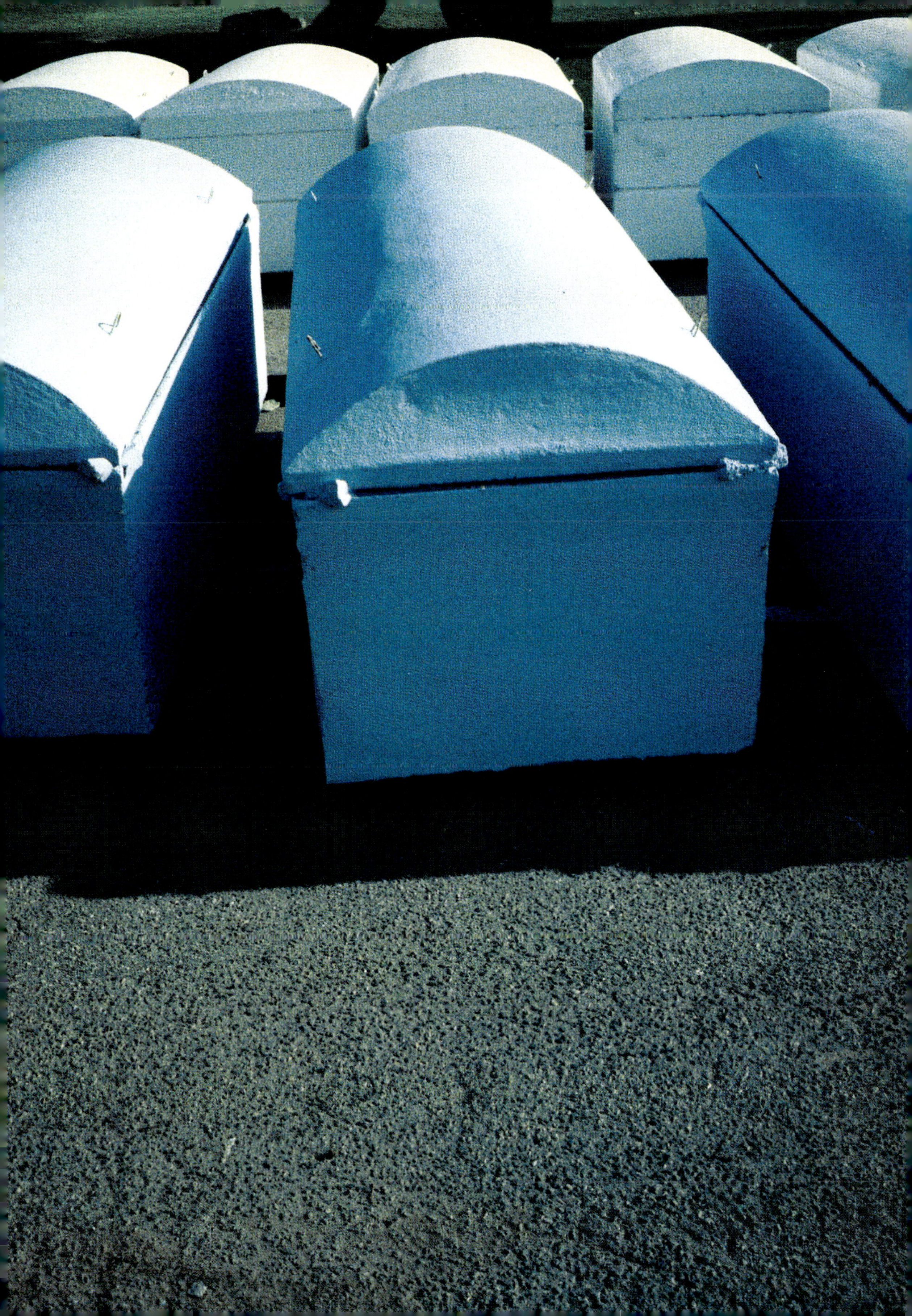

128

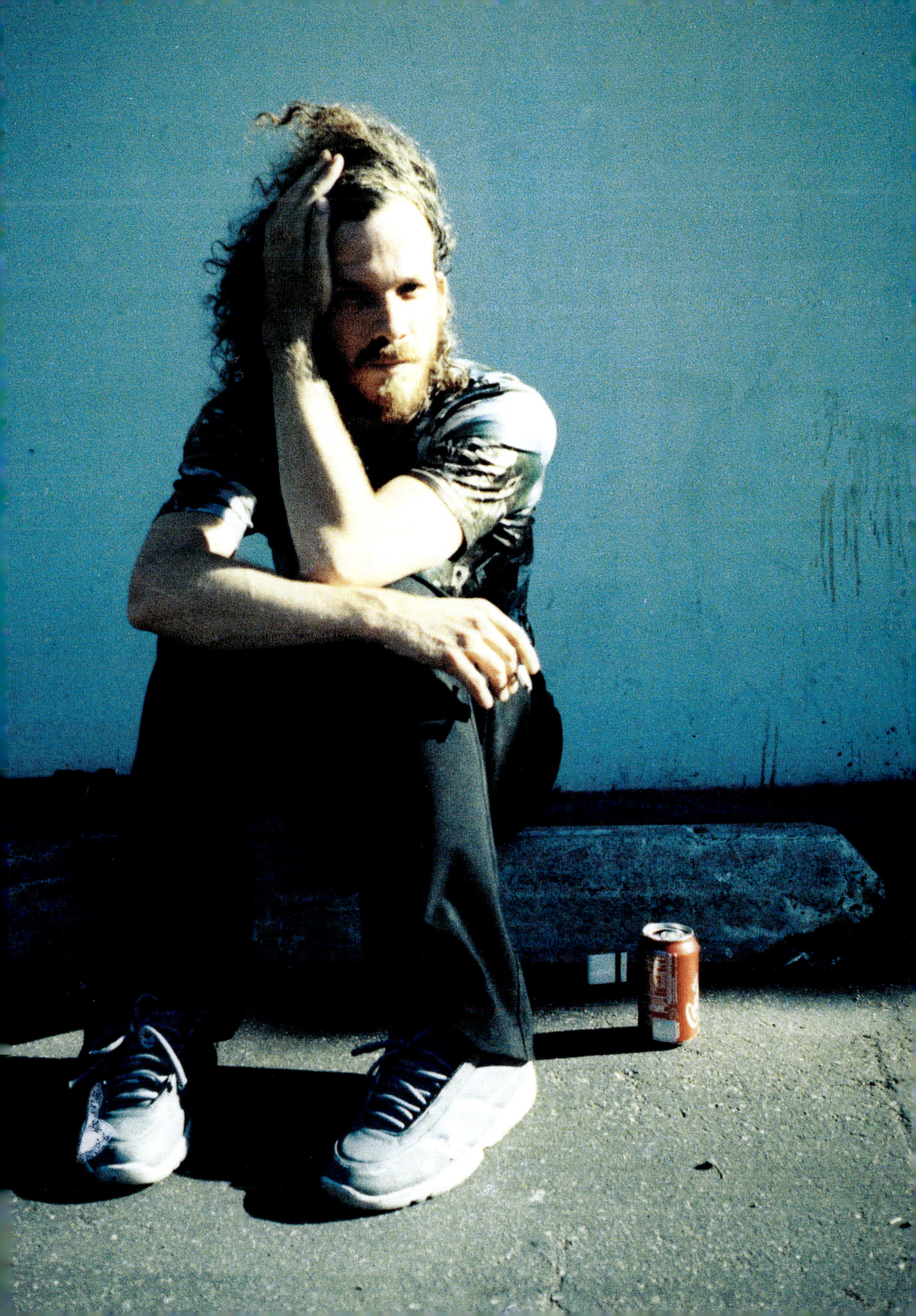

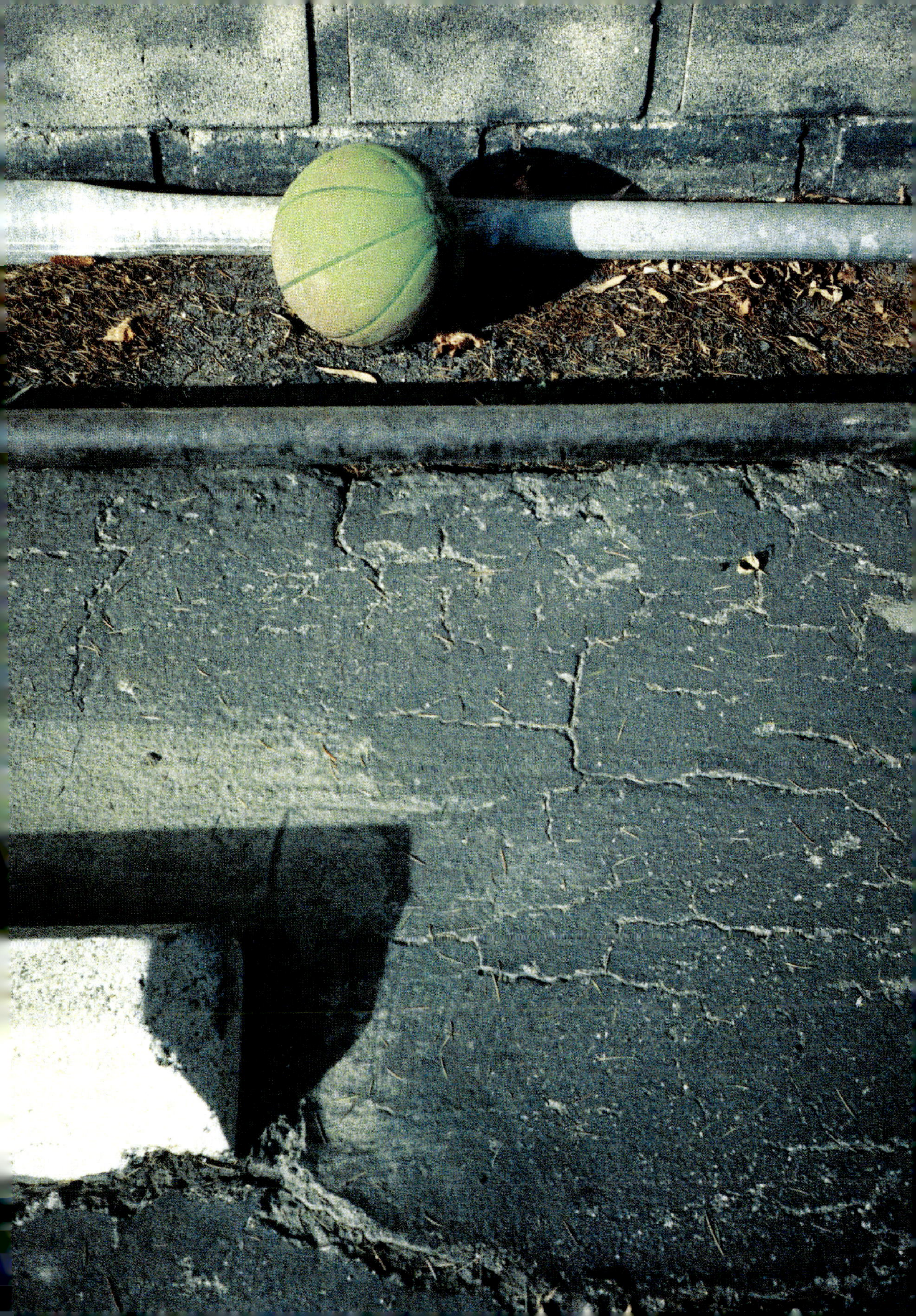

132

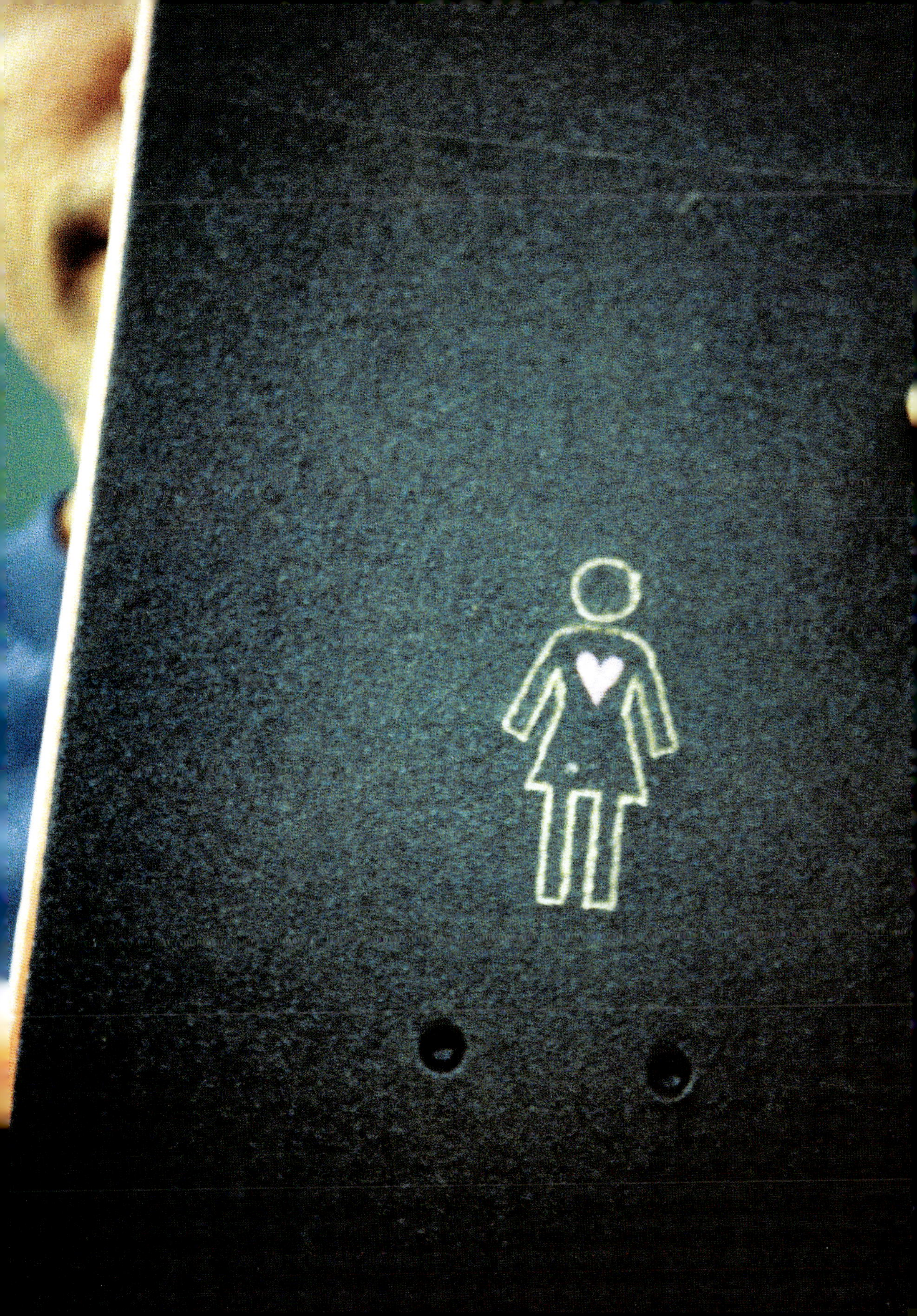

134

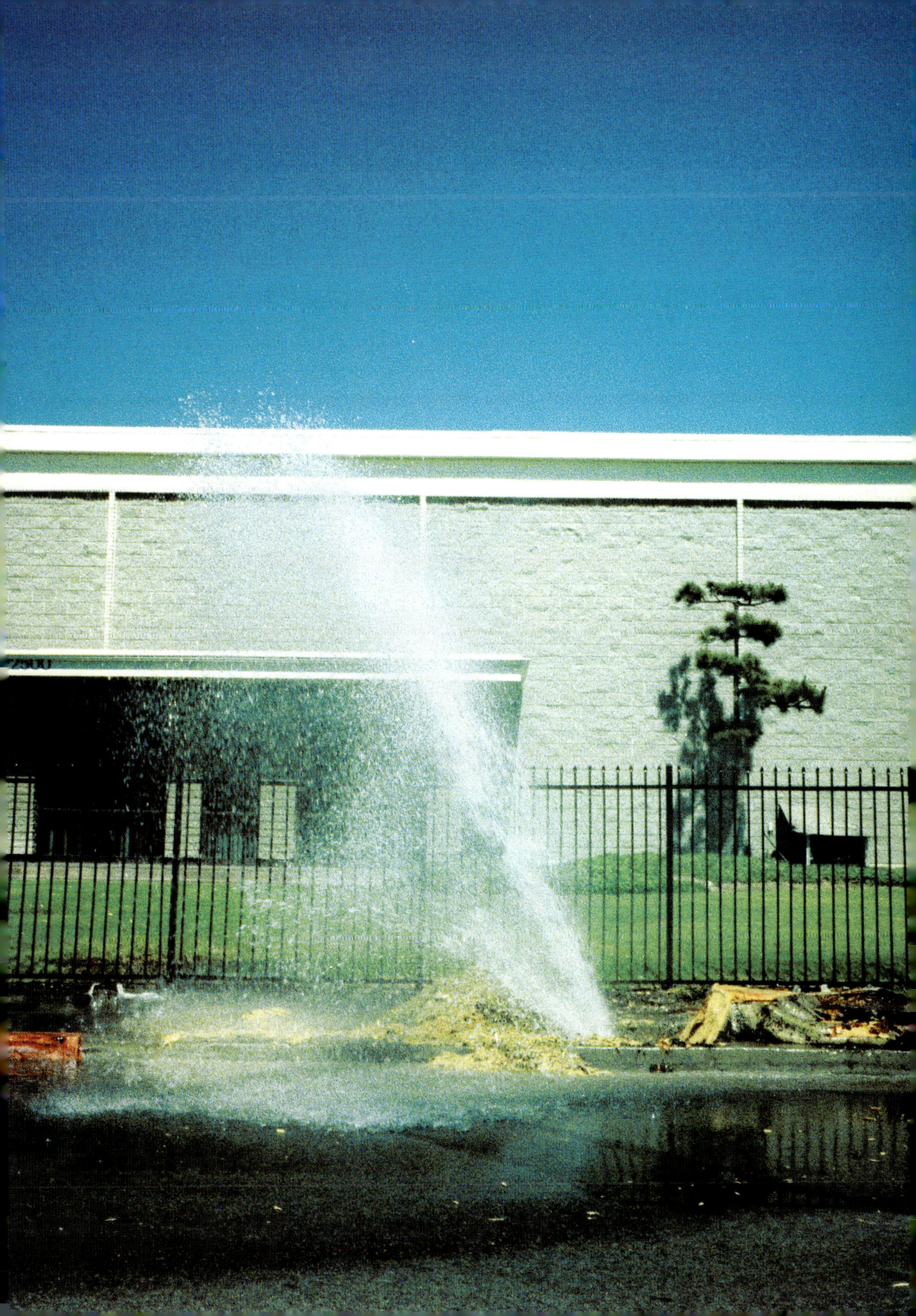

136

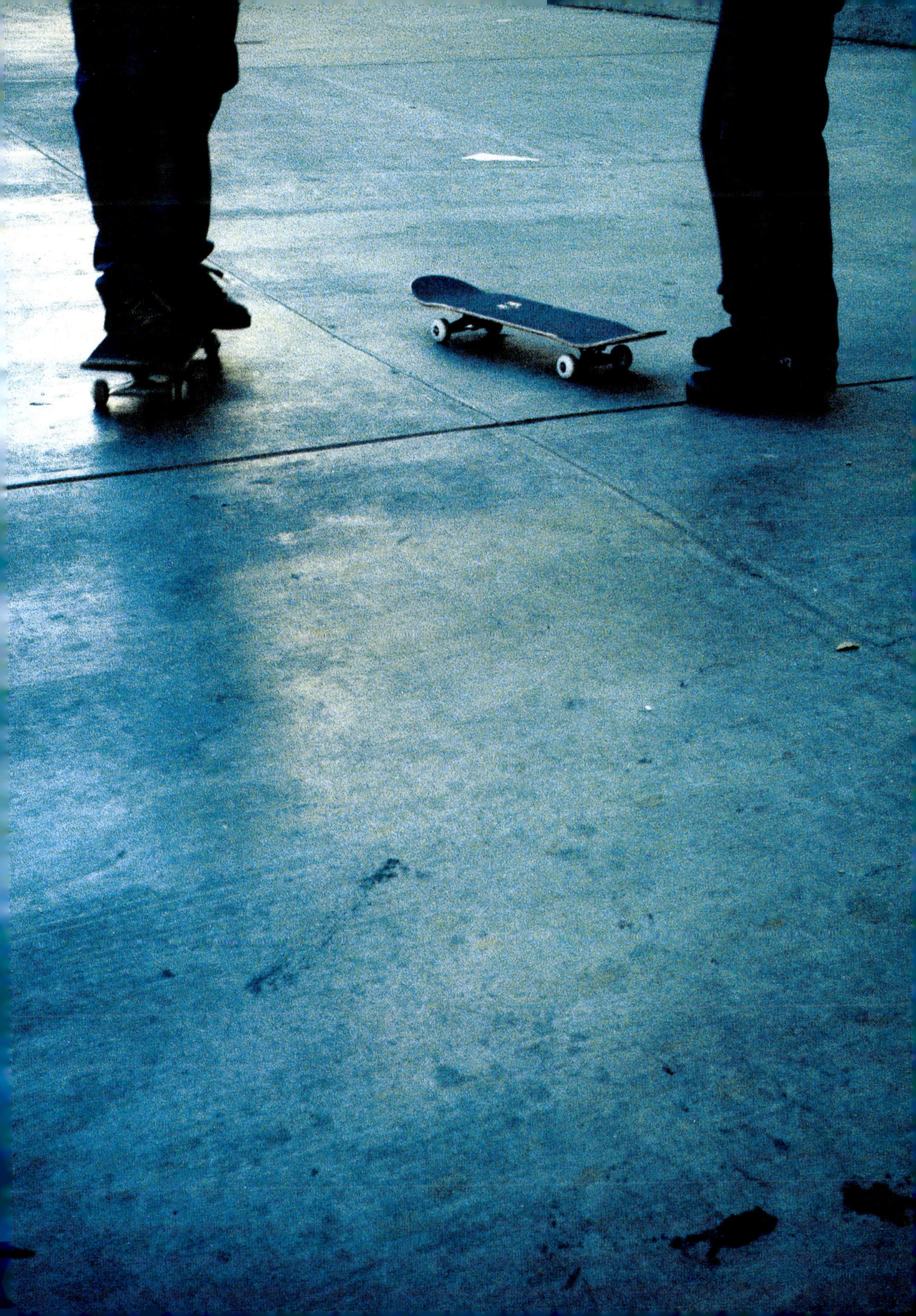

138

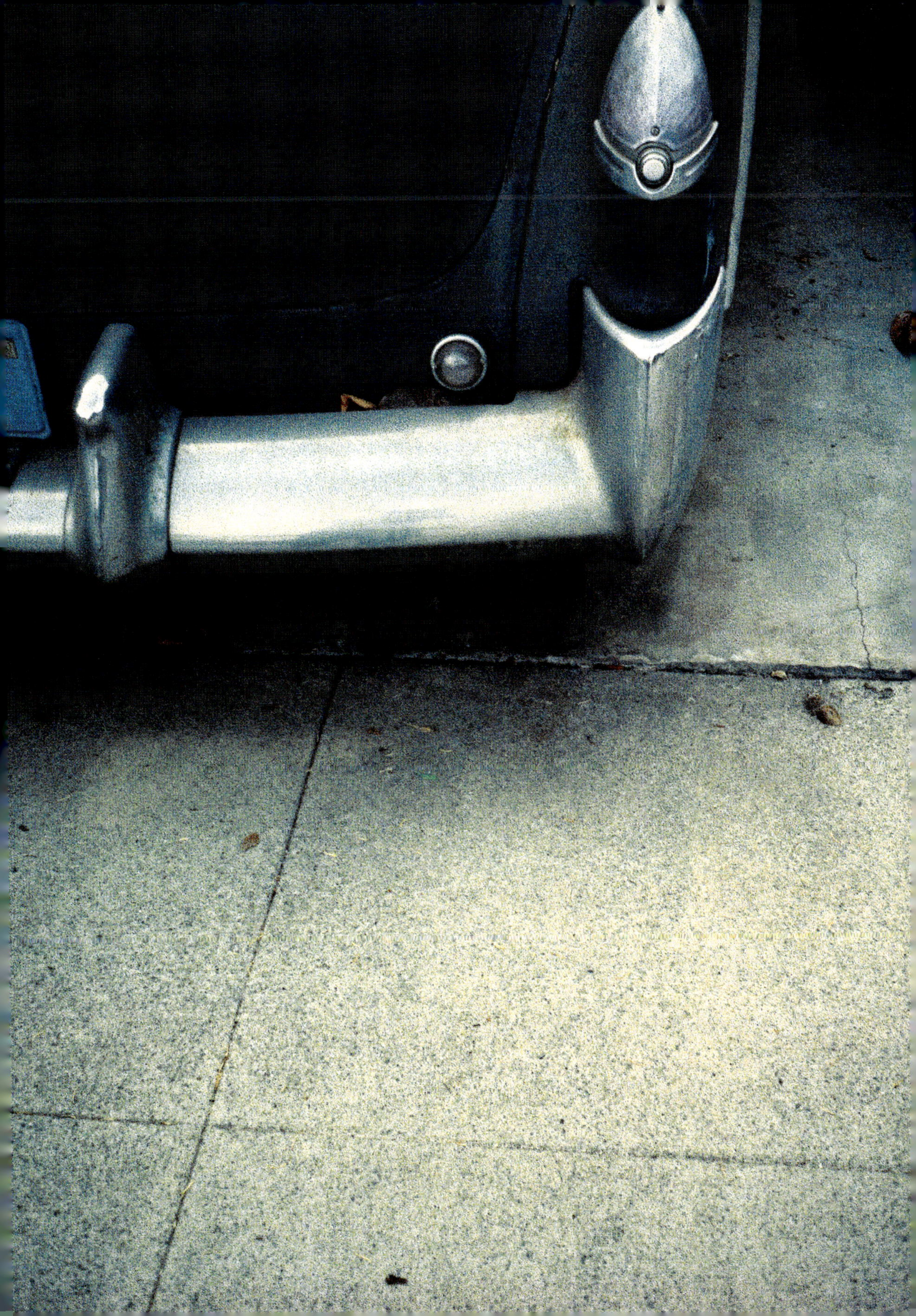

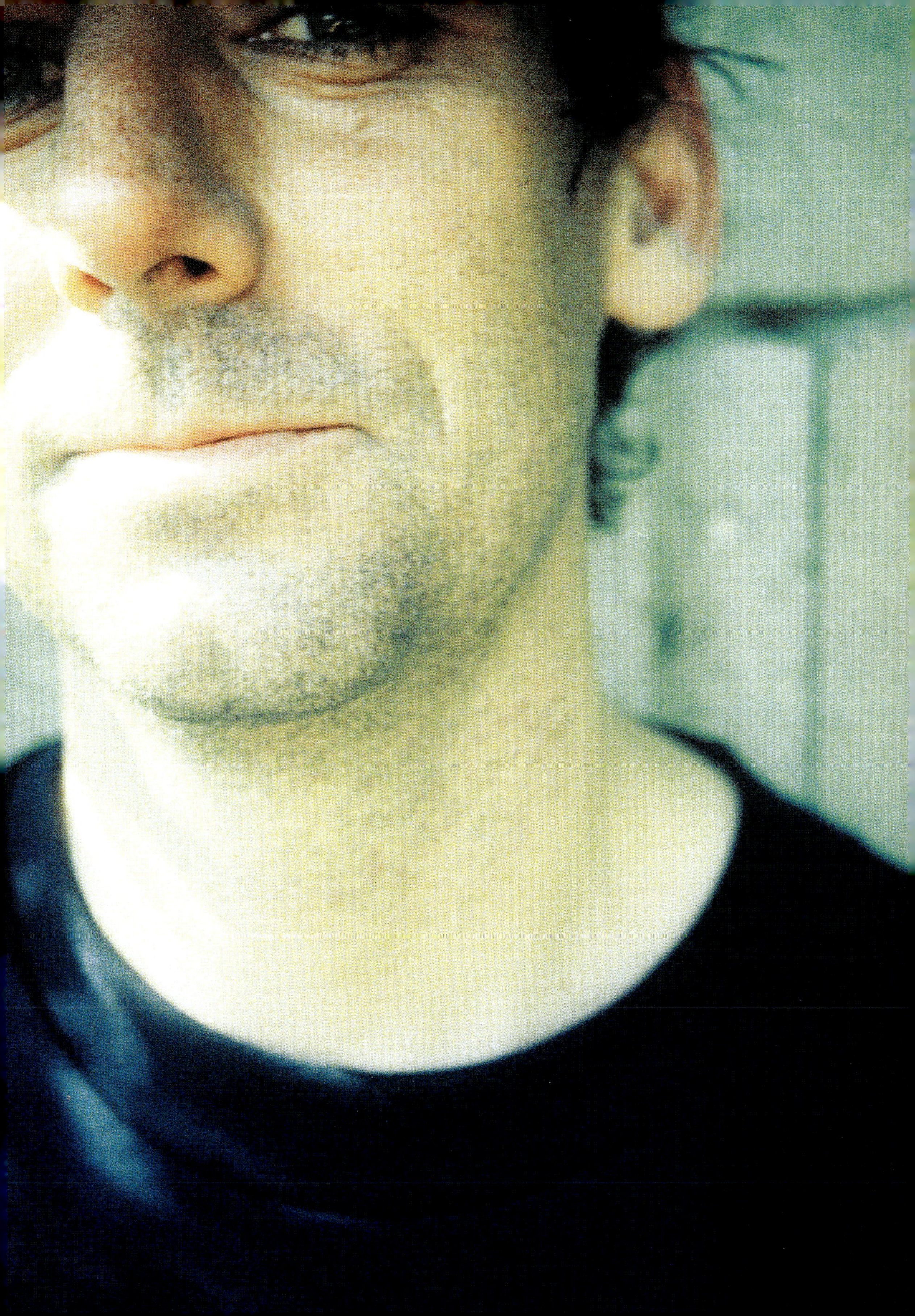

142

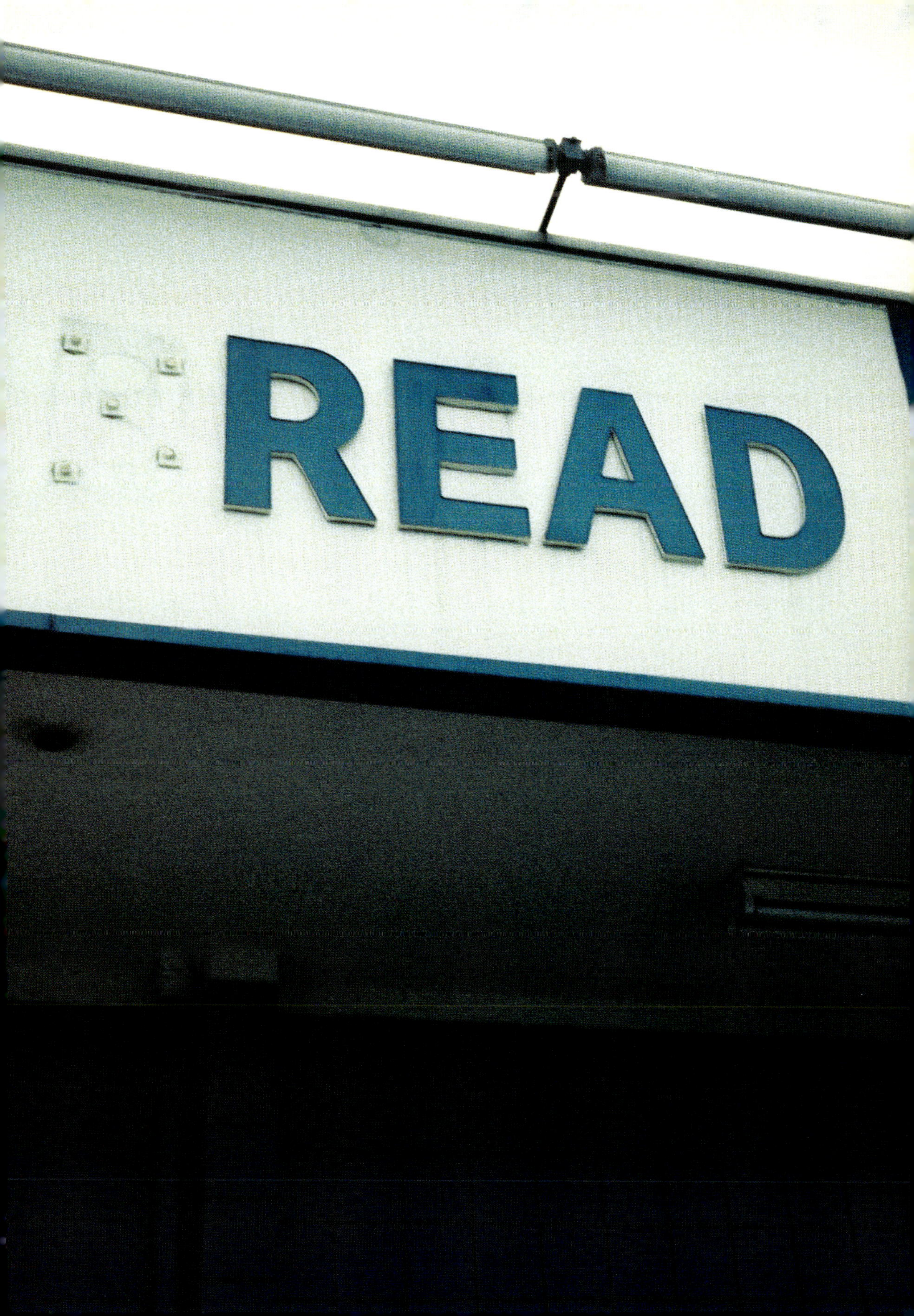
READ

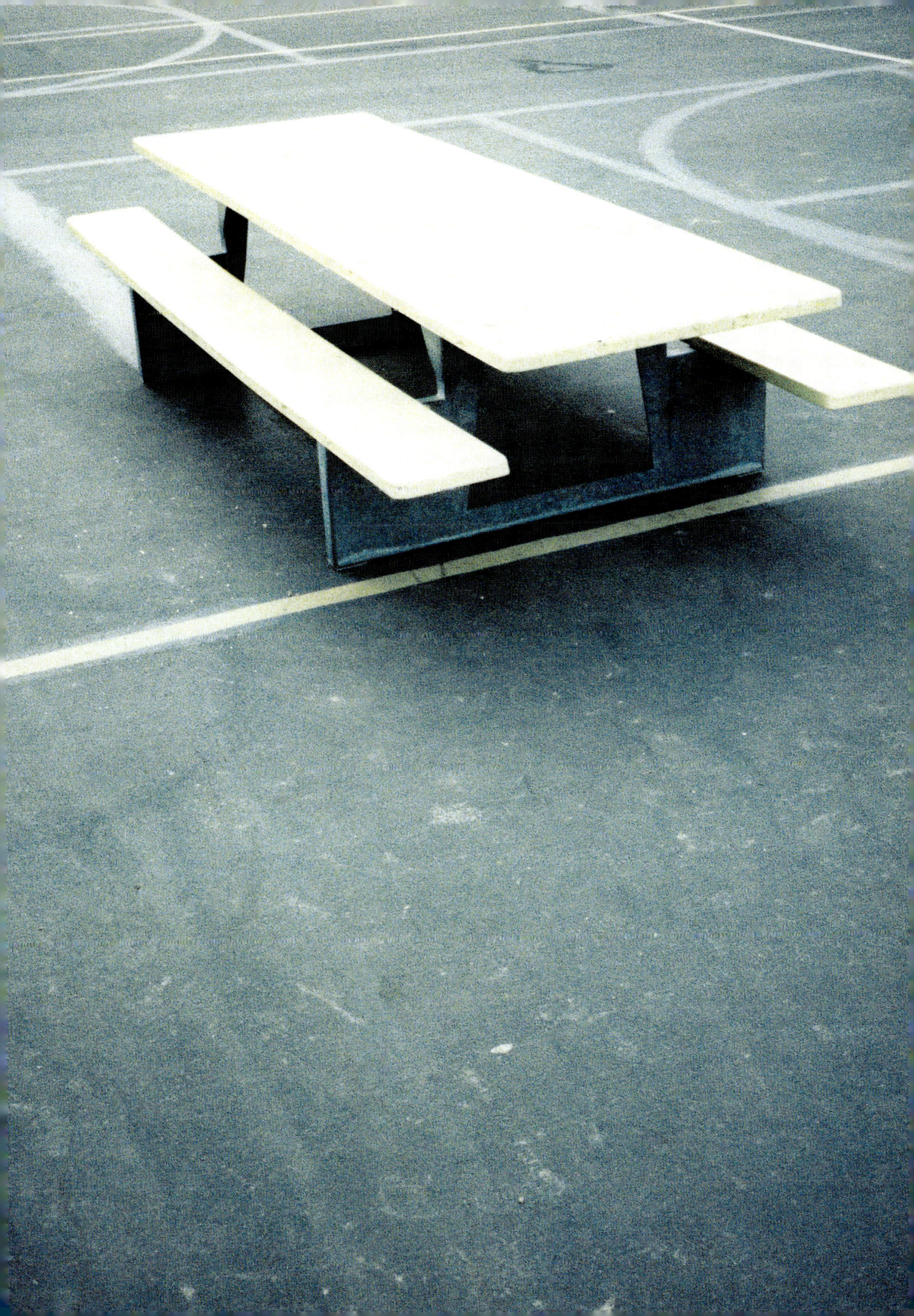

148

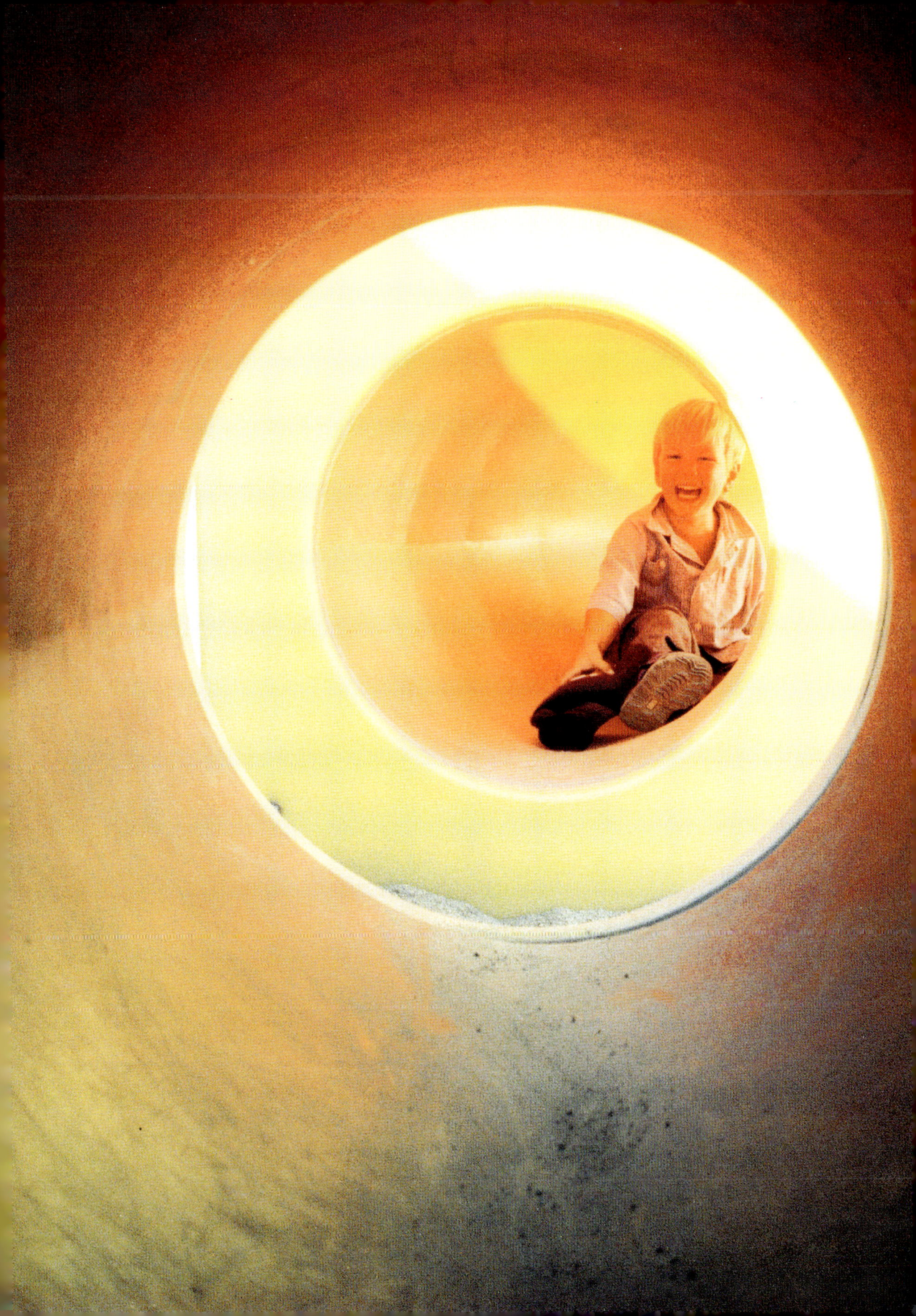

150

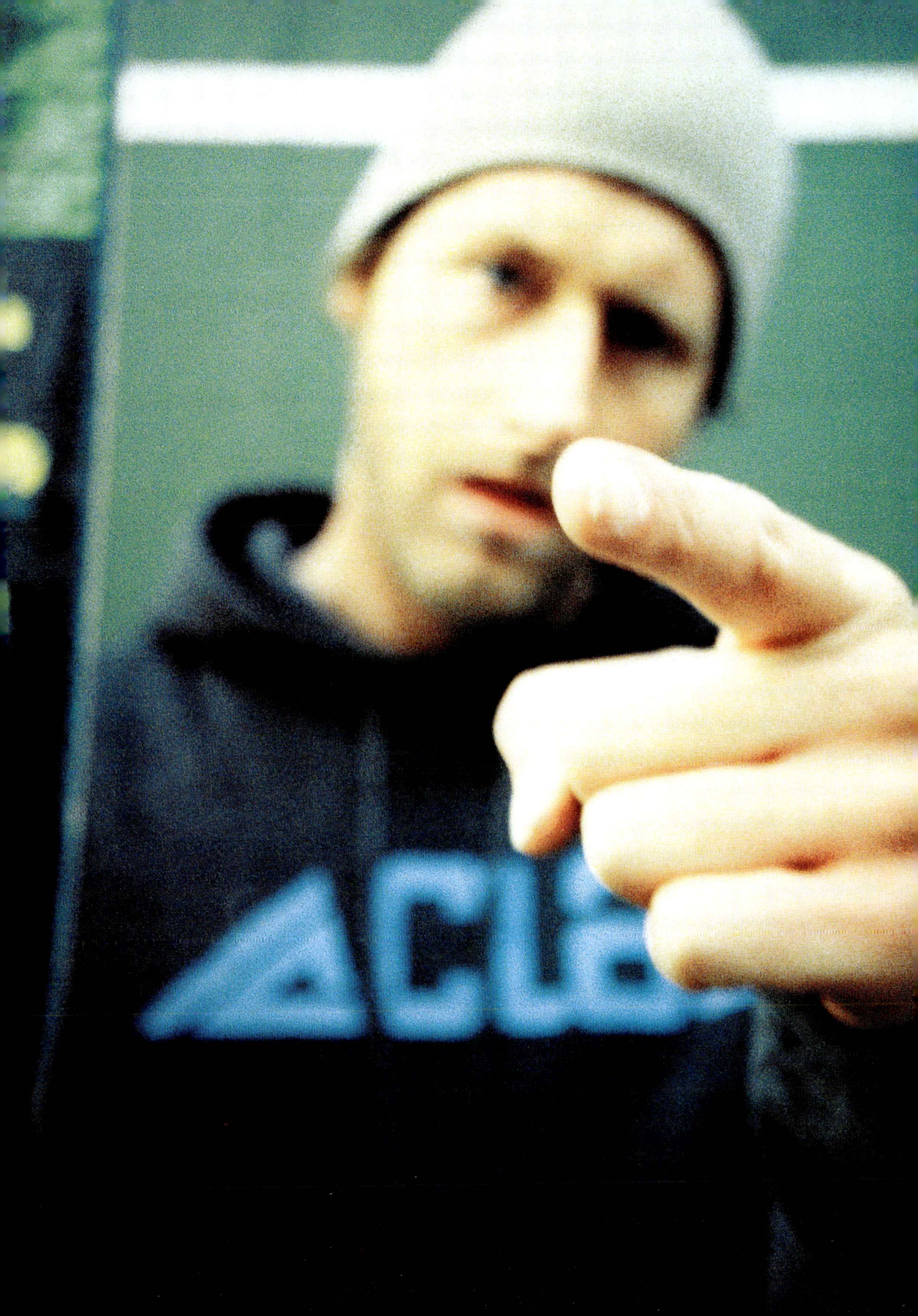

152

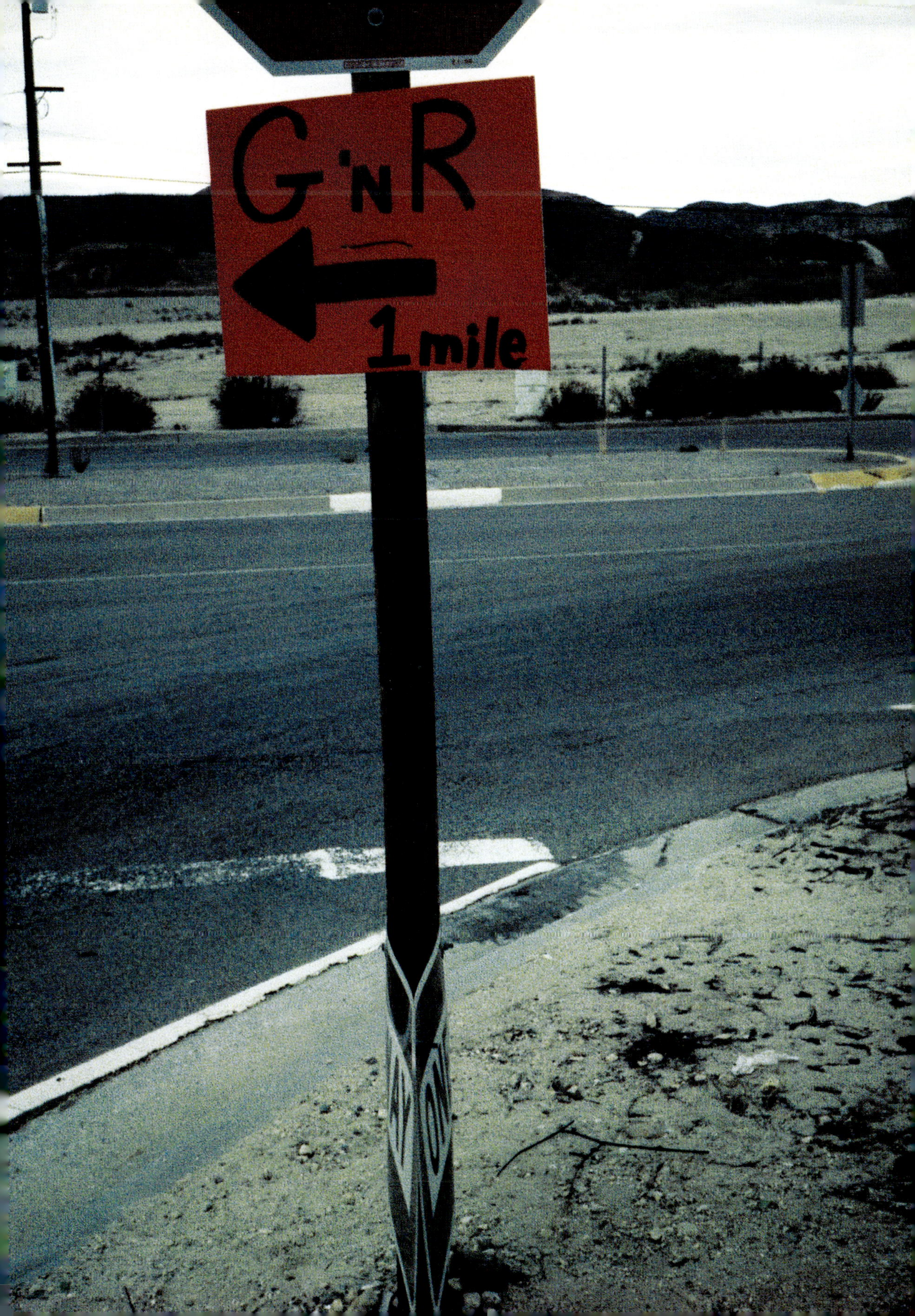
G'N R
1 mile

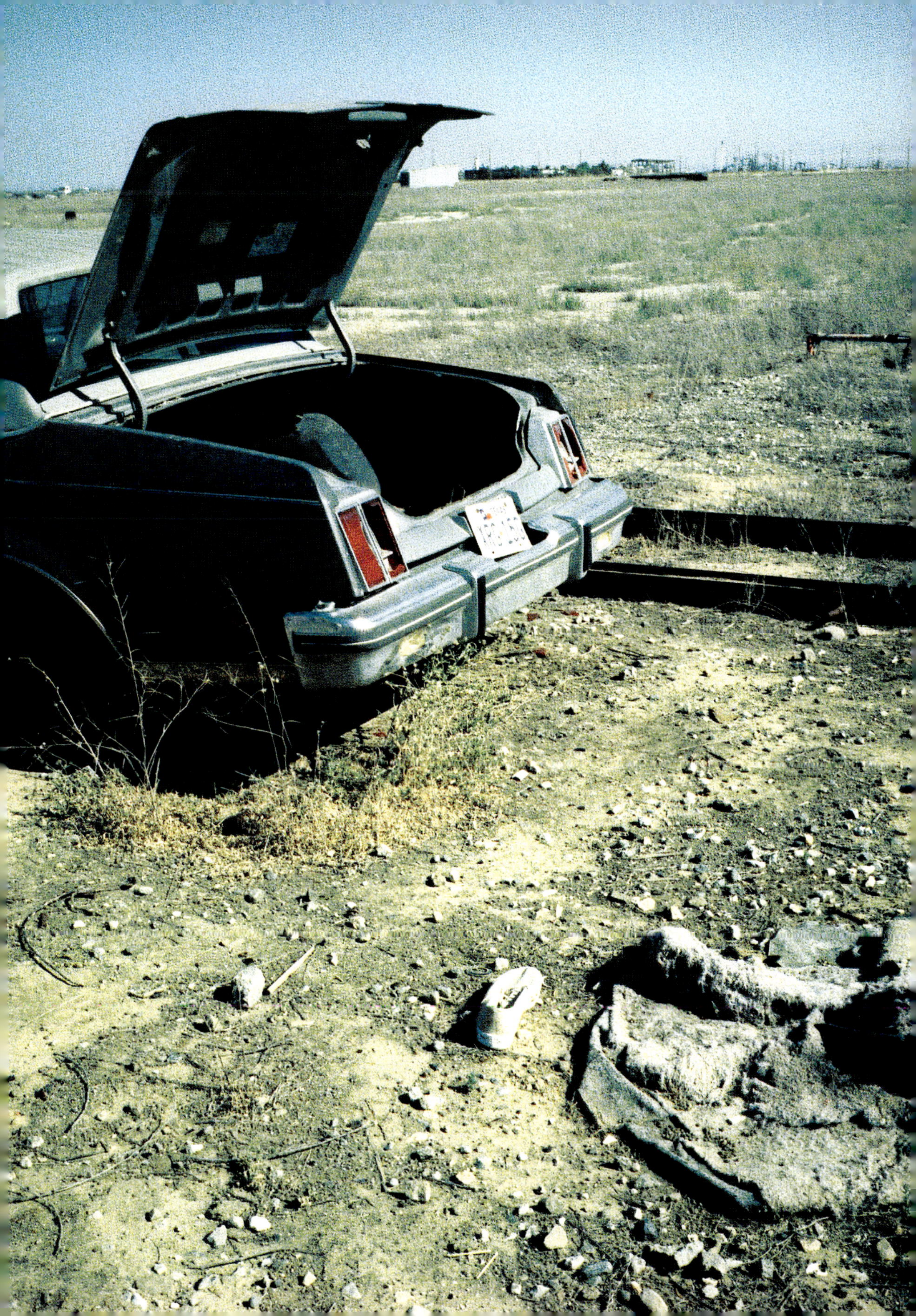

156

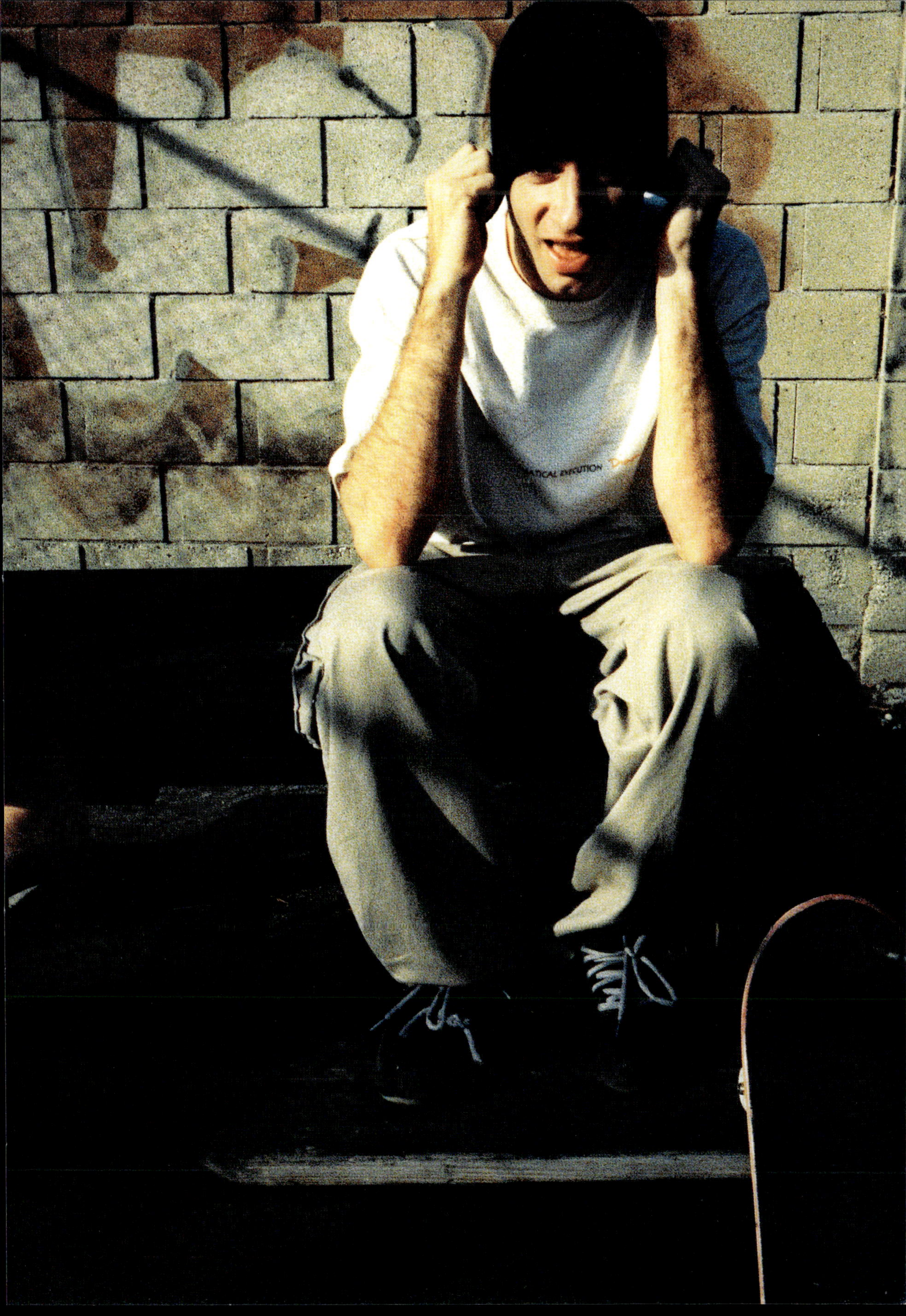

158

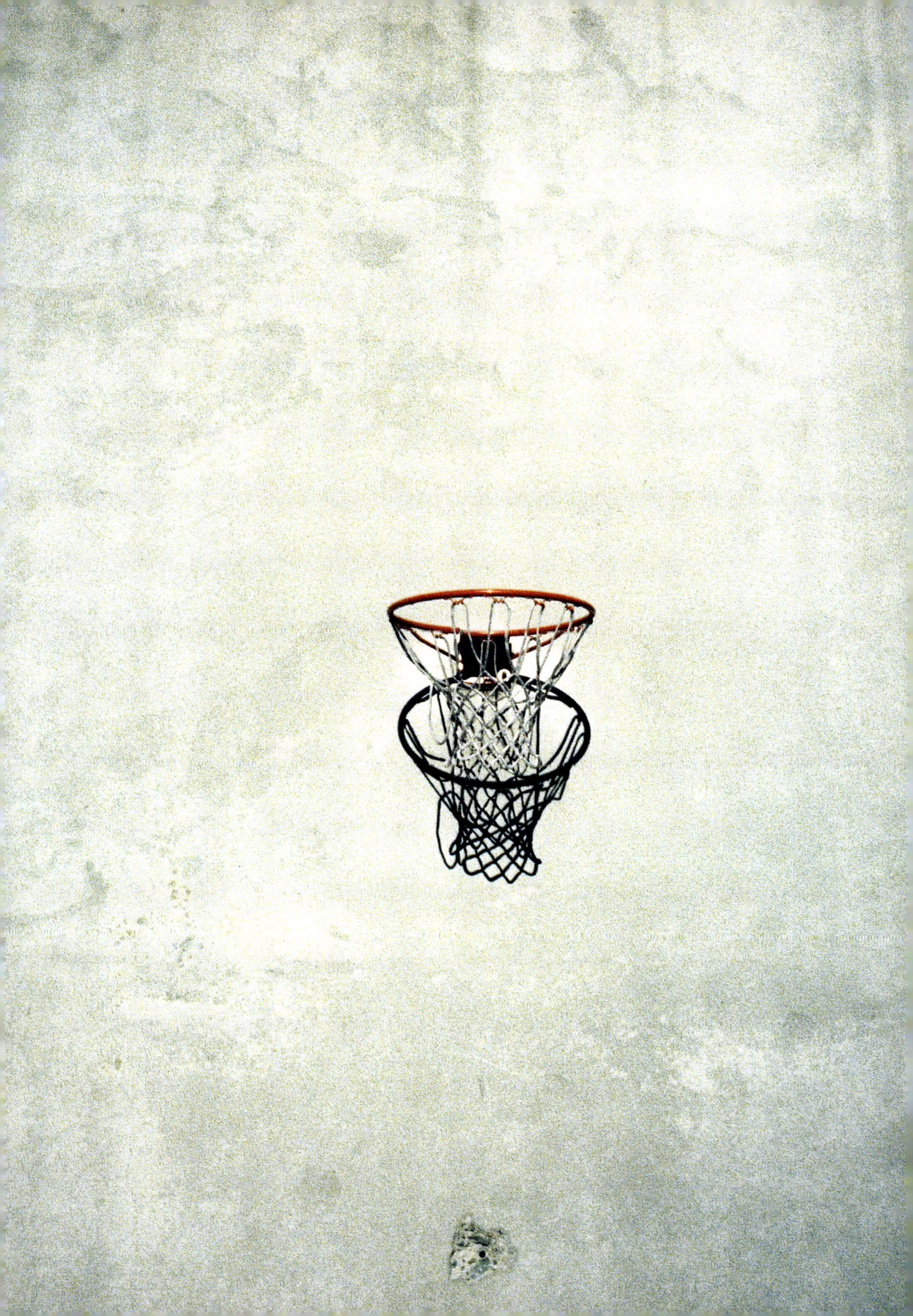

160

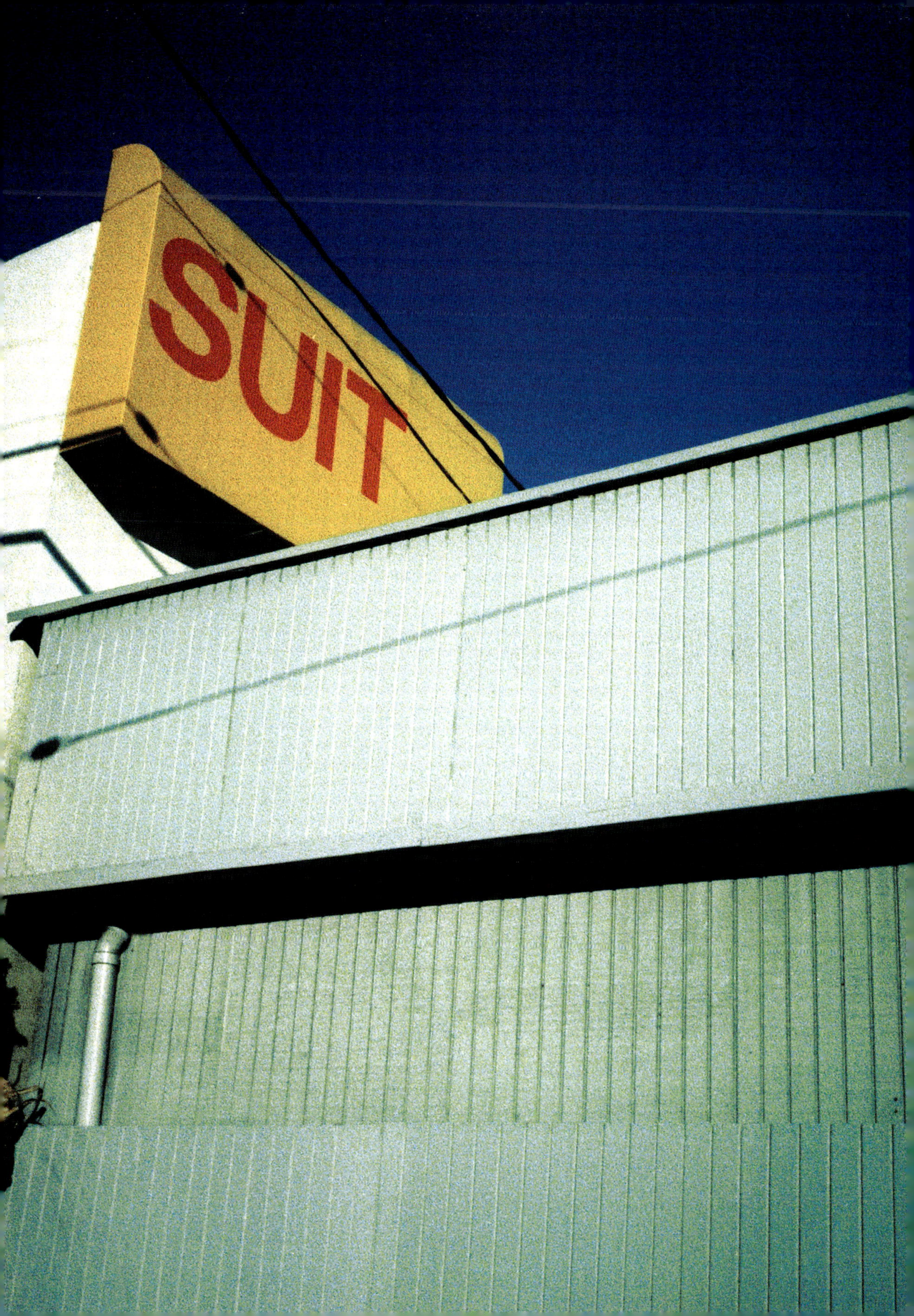
SUIT

164

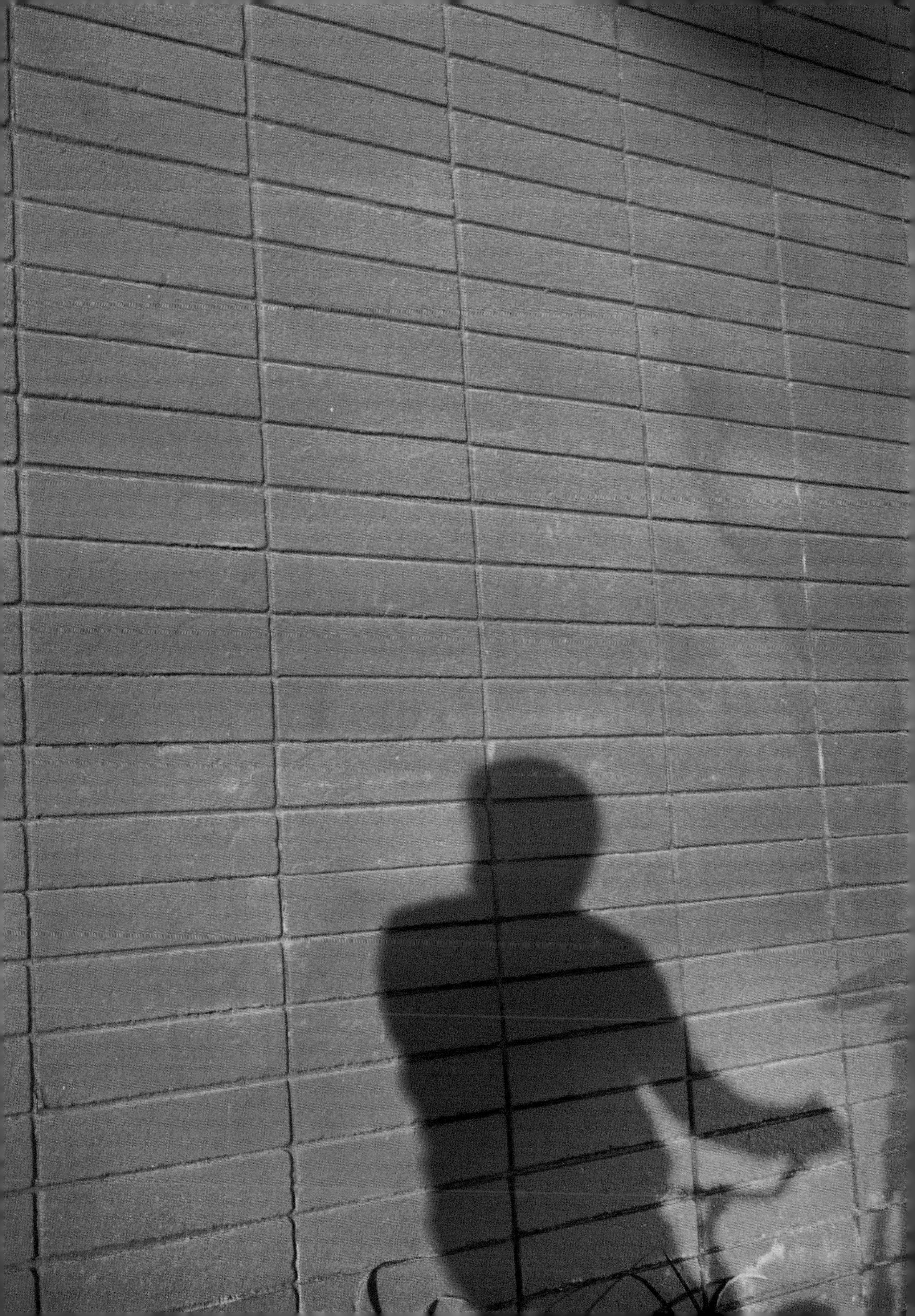

6

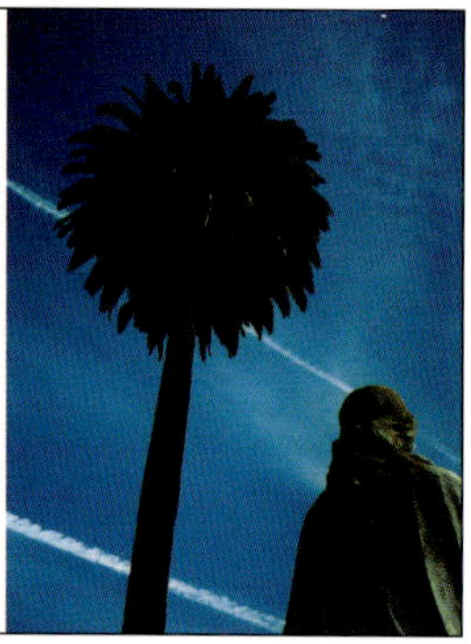

8

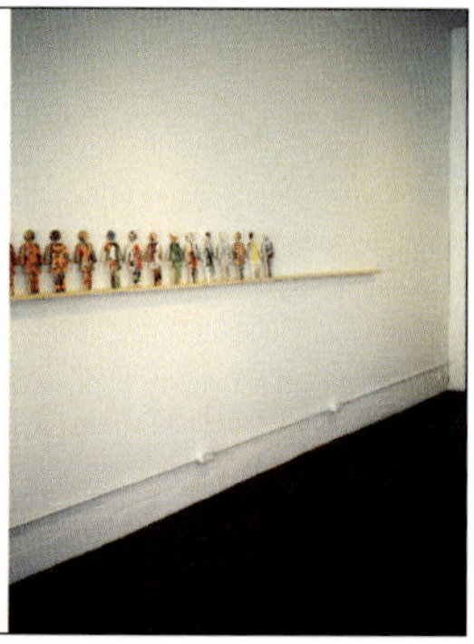

Kenny Anderson
I shot this photo the first time I ever met Kenny and I remember thinking to myself "Man, what a genuine dude". Every time I see him I still think the exact same thing.

10

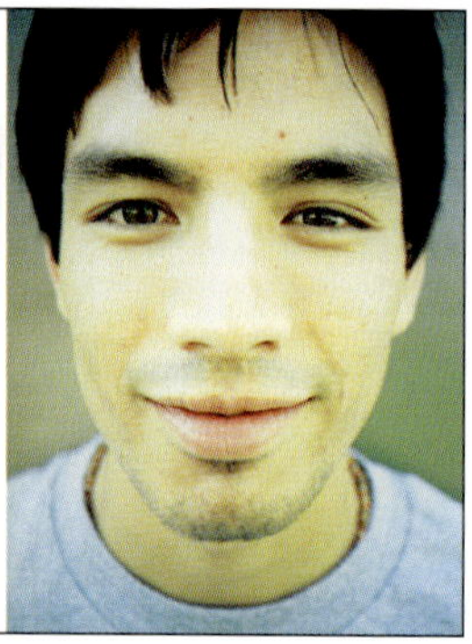

12

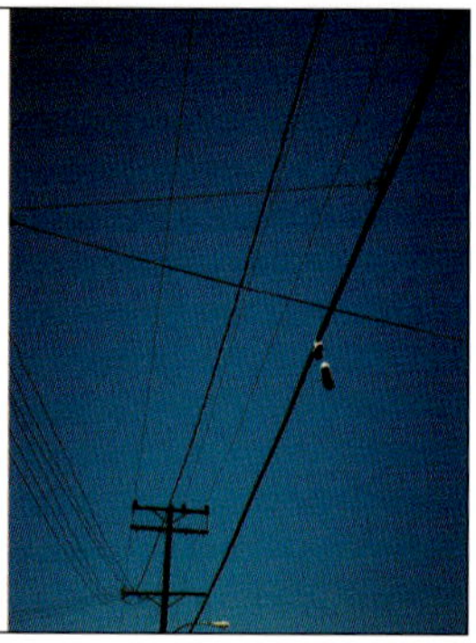

14

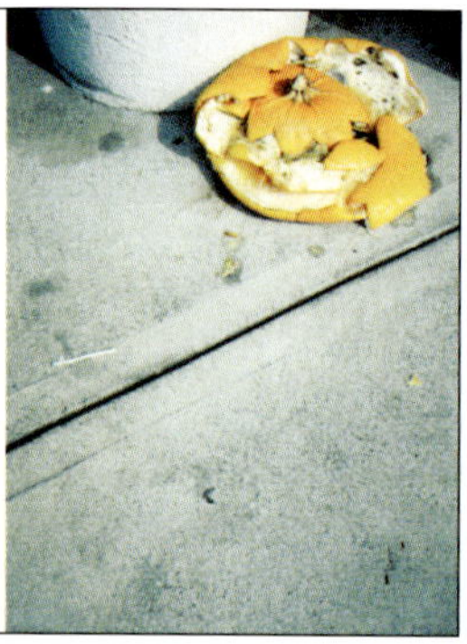

16

Rudy Johnson
I think Rudy is most comfortable with a guitar in his hands. Not that he looks uncomfortable in this photo, but he'd probably look more comfortable strumming away at something.

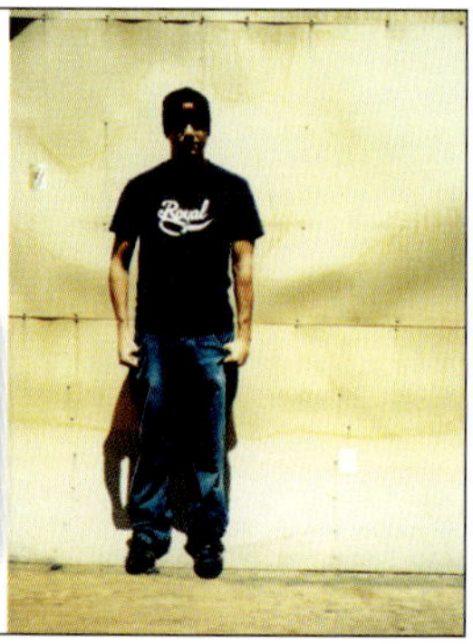

18

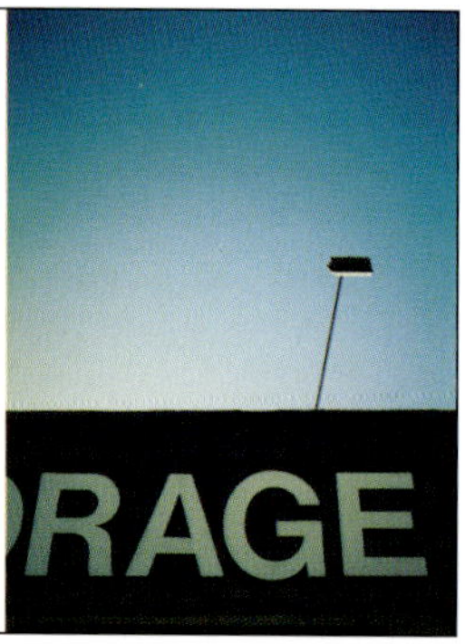

20

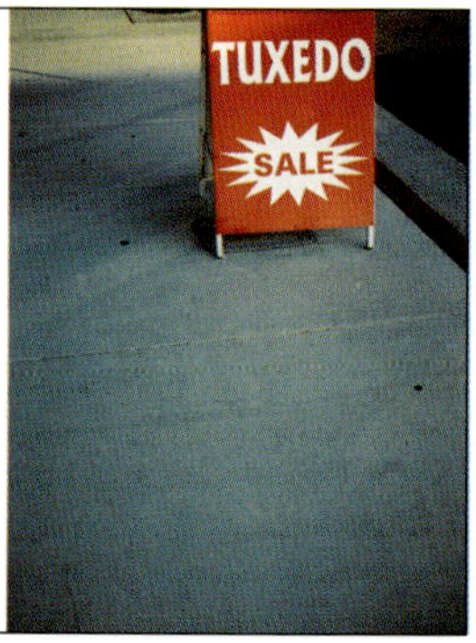

22

Nick Tershay
Nick is one of those people who you work with and you don't realize how rad he is until you're not around him anymore. One day he decided to design a t-shirt that had a gun silk screened on it near the waist. It never got released but he's pictured here wearing the prototype.

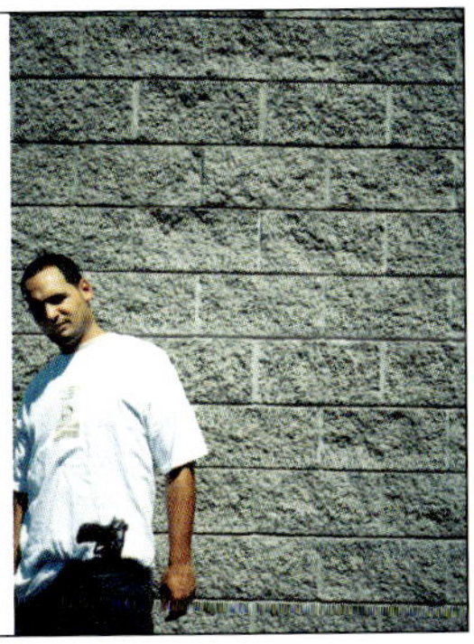

24

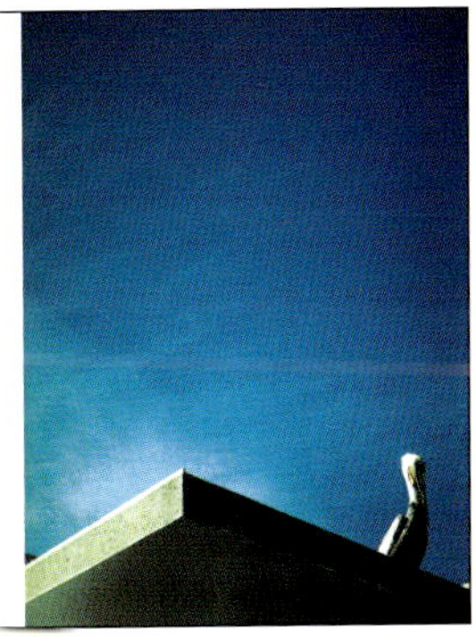

26

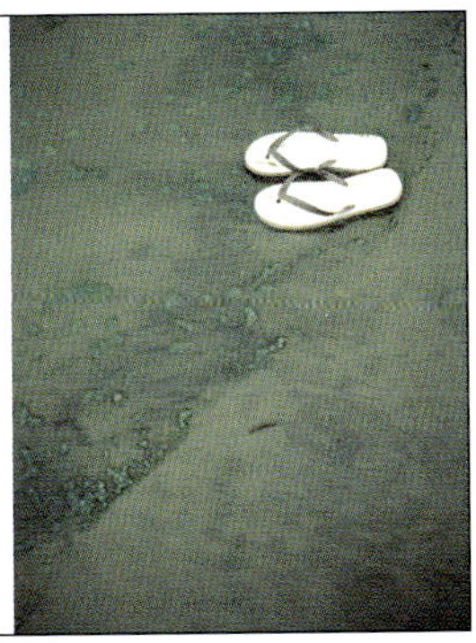

28

Lori D
Lori D and I have the same belt and the same penchant for buying rad fruit at roadside fruit stands on the way to Pismo Beach.

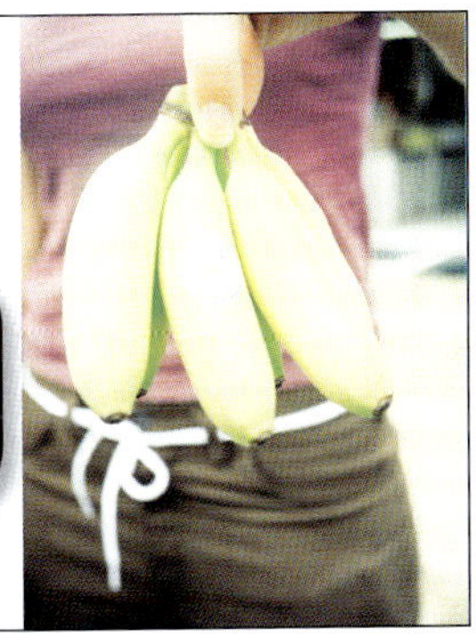

30

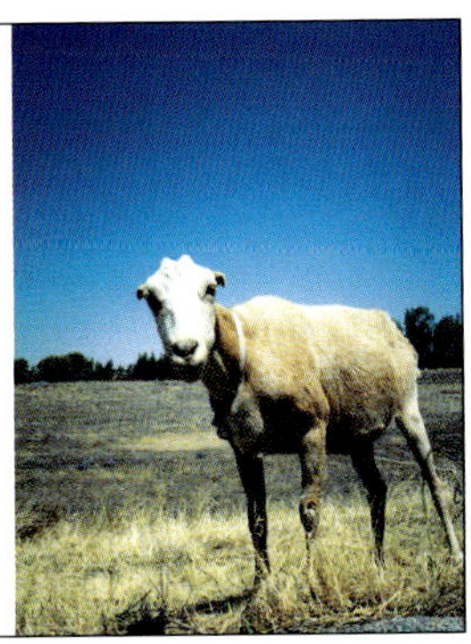

32

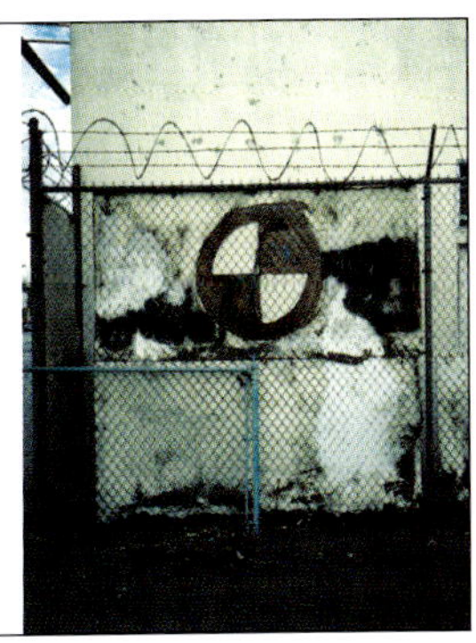

34

Andy Jenkins
On any Sunday, Jenkins can be seen racing motorcycles on dirt tracks in the middle of nowhere. This one is his son's and he's pictured riding it in a parking lot in Torrance. Not quite a dirt track but oh well.

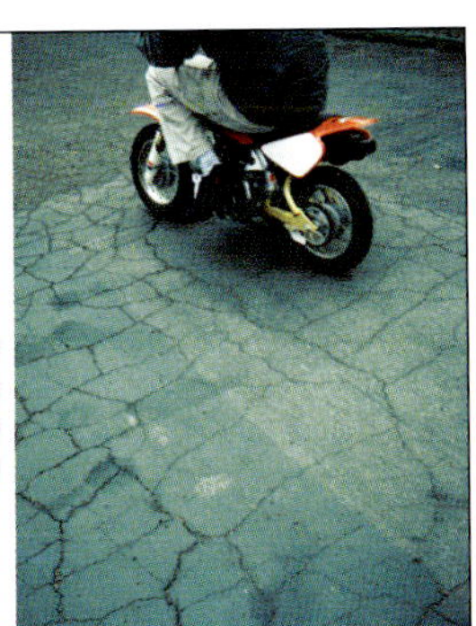

Andy Jenkins
This close up photo once showed up in *Nickelodeon* magazine. Random, but I think the image captures a true essence of Jenkins.

36

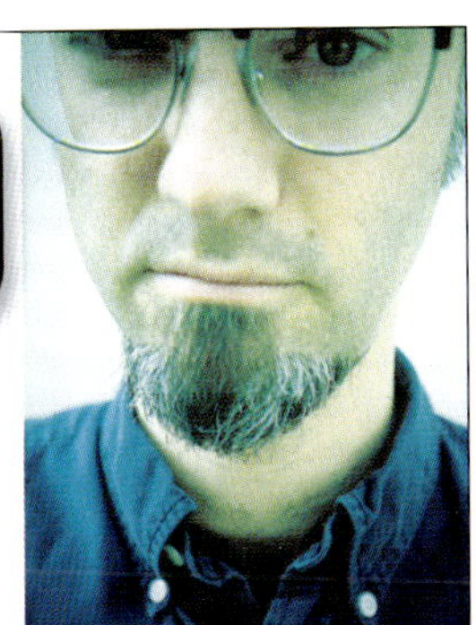

38

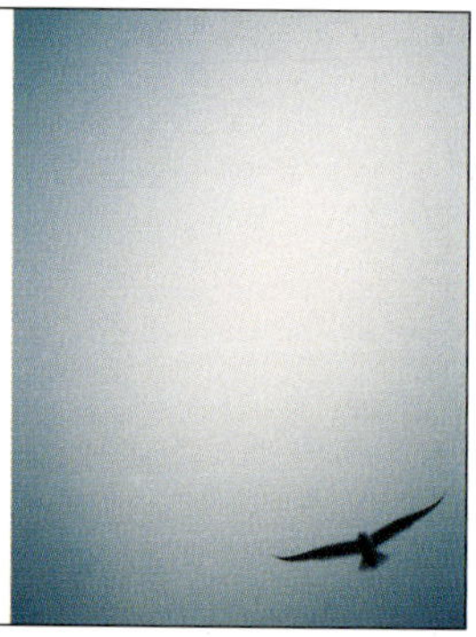

40

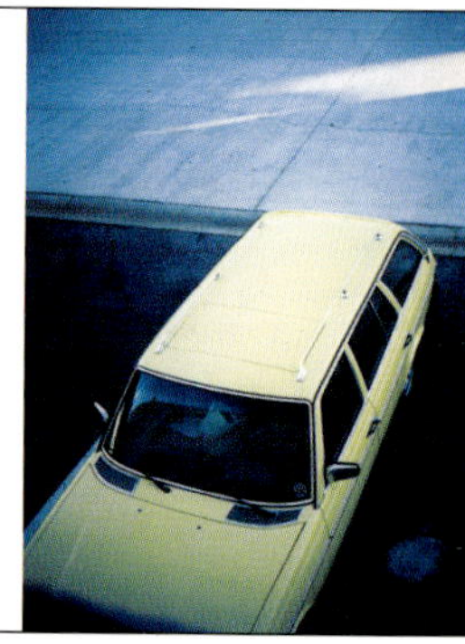

42

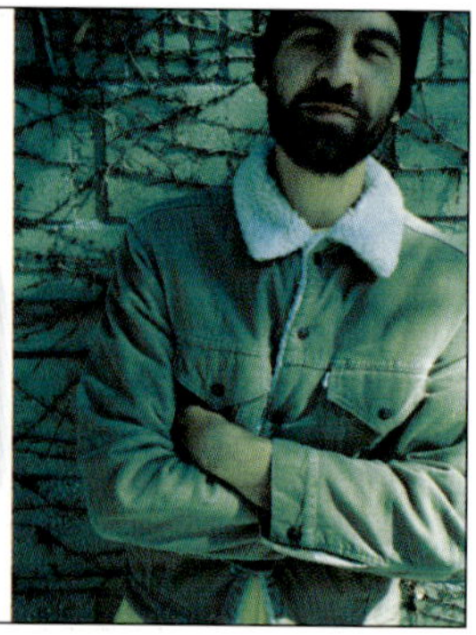

Michael Leon
Michael hates getting his photo taken and he hates looking at photos of himself. When I showed him this one he said "Hm, I don't mind it" and I was flattered.

44

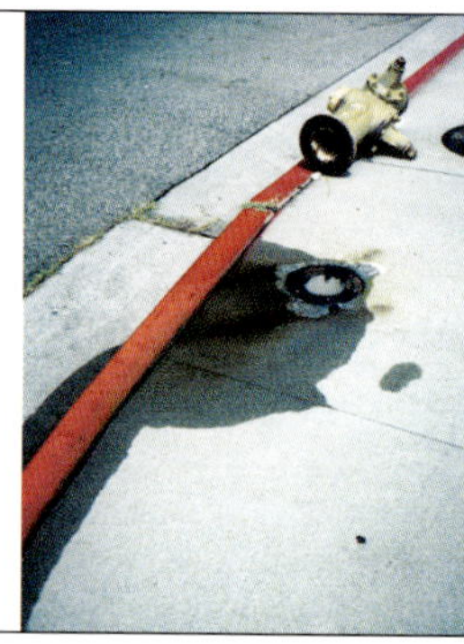

46

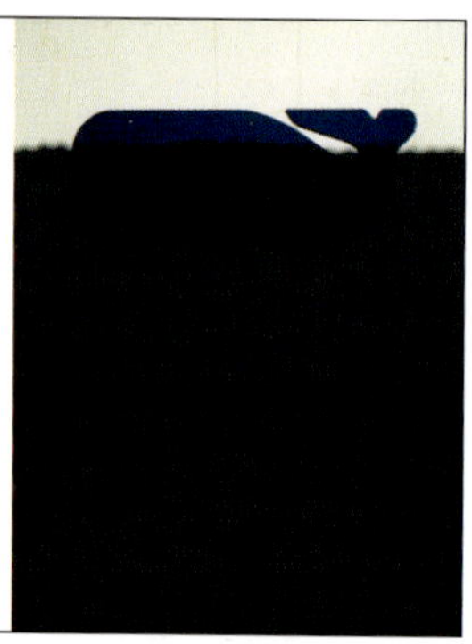

48

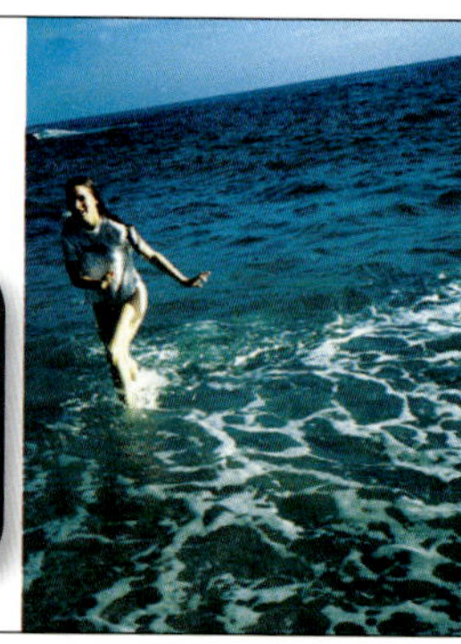

Rebecca Shlien
It is a fairly common assumption that 95% of the photographs that a male photographer takes of women are of his girlfriend or wife. This is not the only photo I took of my ex-girlfriend, Rebecca, but it's one of my favorites.

50

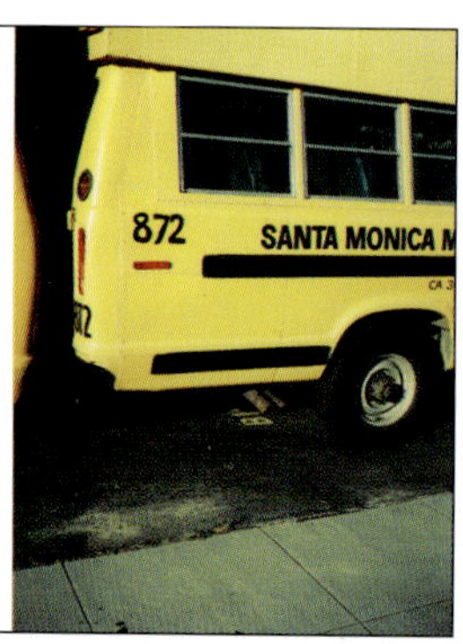

52

54

Chris Roberts
I watched the final Lakers game of the season at Chris's house this year. He was wearing the same colored wristbands but unfortunately the mood wasn't quite as festive as it was in this photo, taken a couple of days after the last time they won a ring.

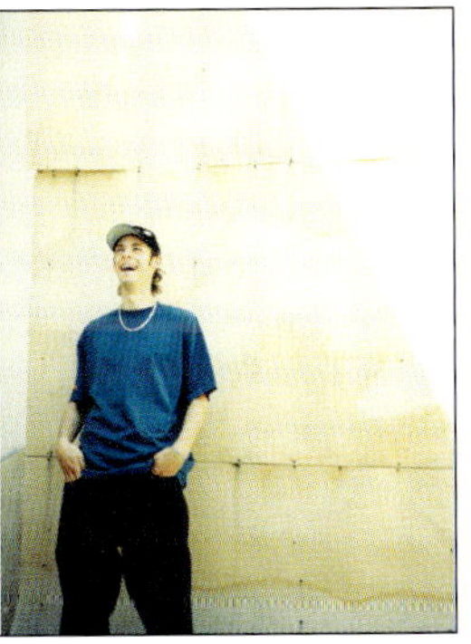

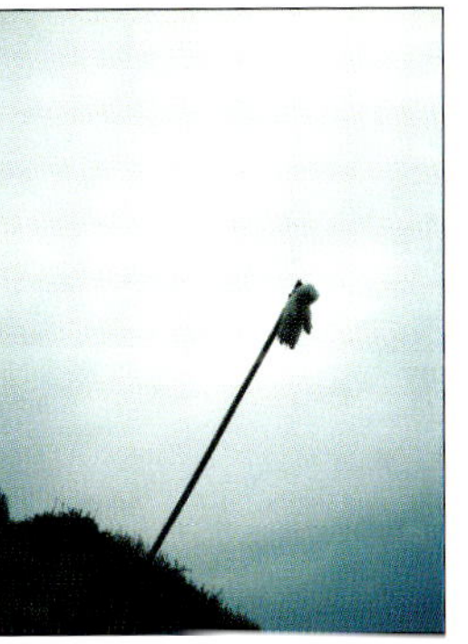

56

Brad Staba and Marc Johnson
It would appear as though Brad's a dick and Marc's a ball.

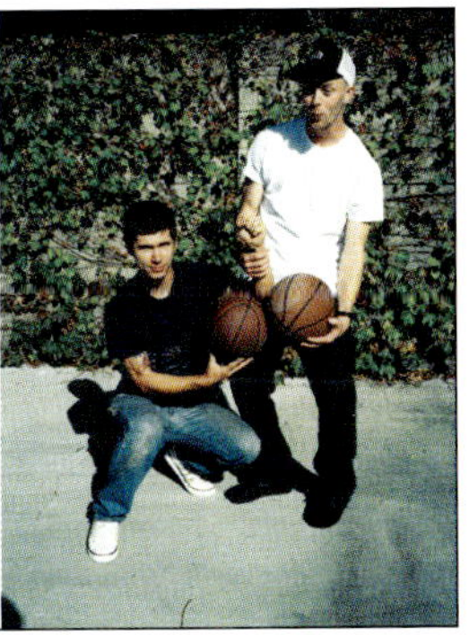

58

60

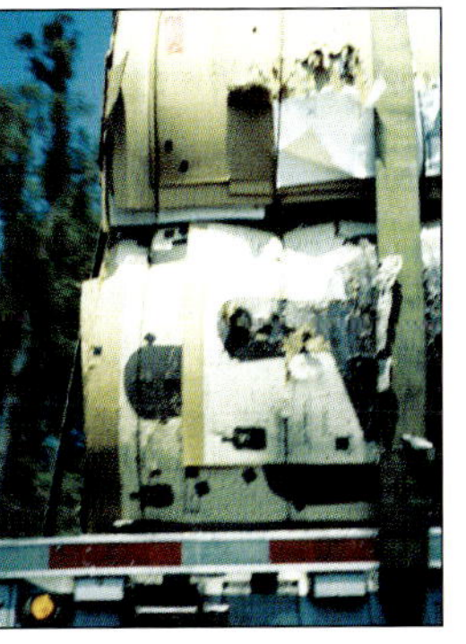

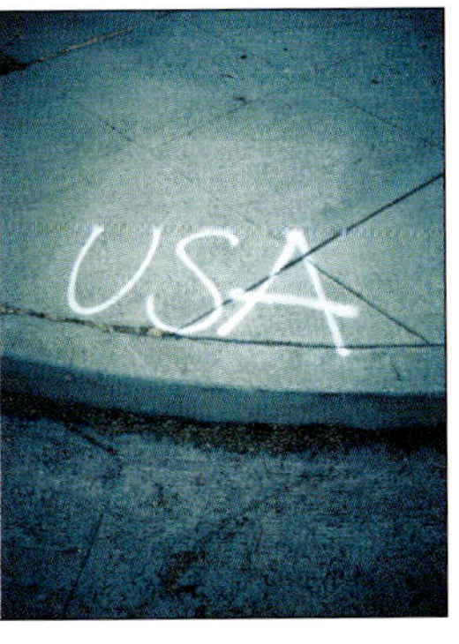

62

64

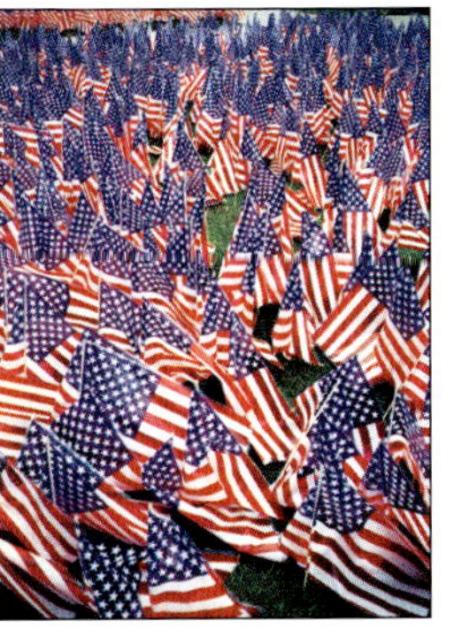

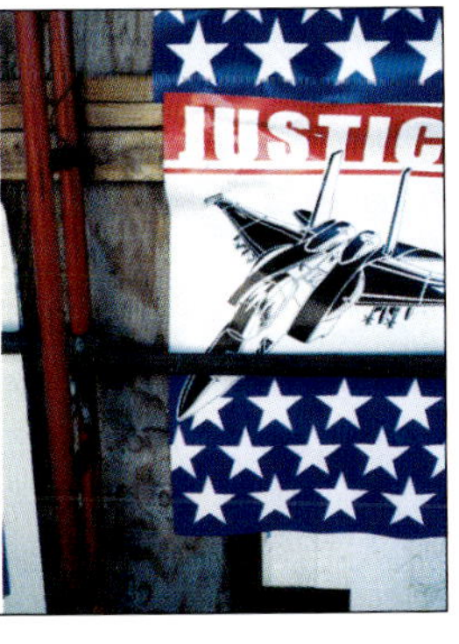

66

68

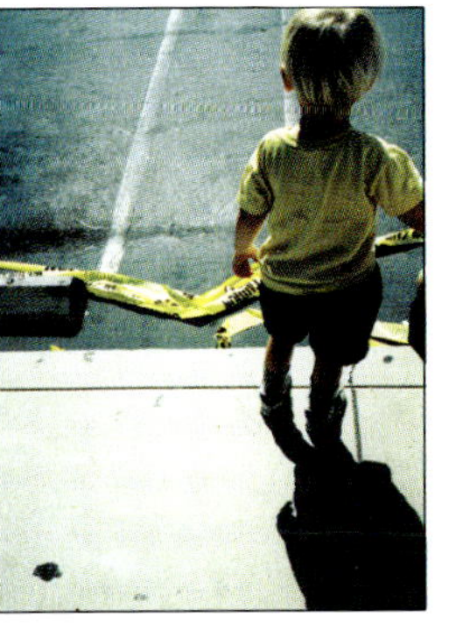

70

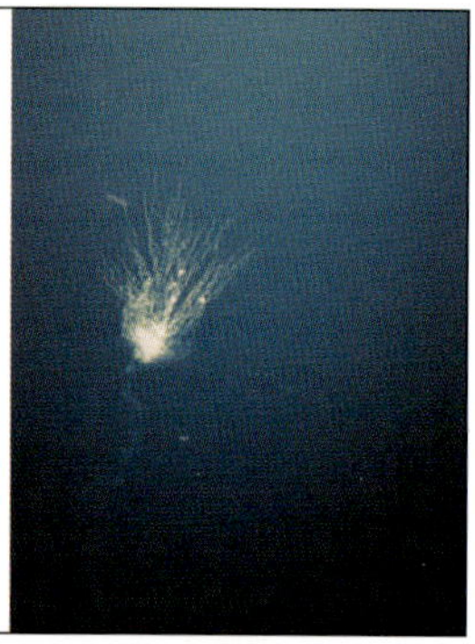

72

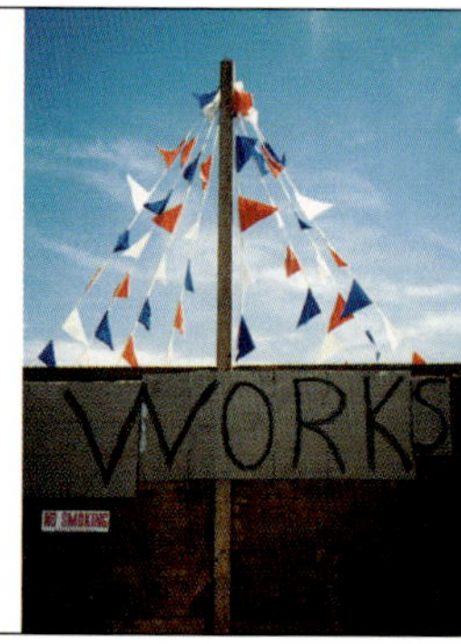

Rick Howard
Jenkins can probably be seen riding on more Sundays than Rick, but Rick definitely gives him a run for his money.

74

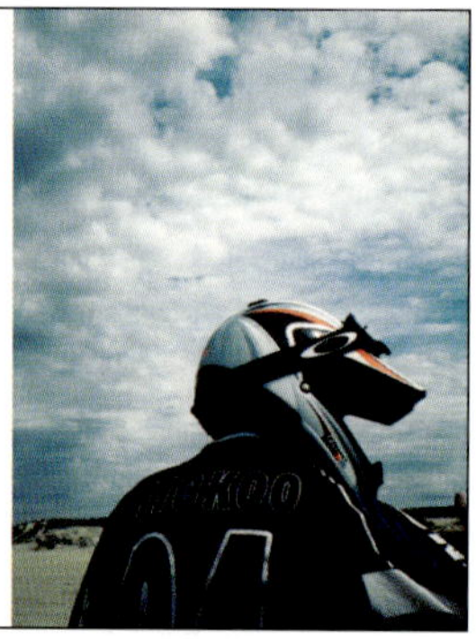

76

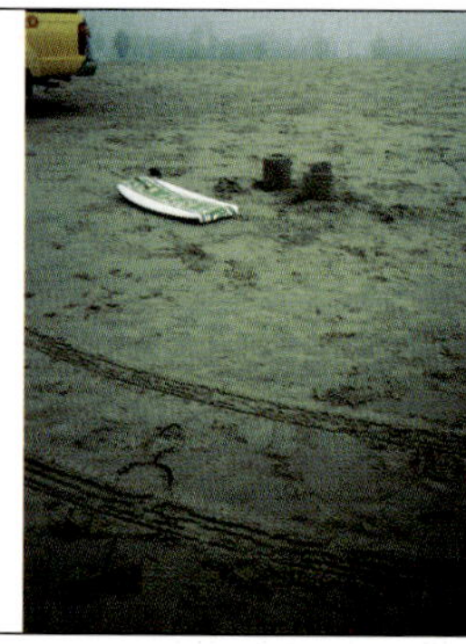

Mike Carroll
"Do I have something in my eye?", "How do I get it out?", "What if it's something gnarly?", "Can I get sick from it?". Mike is a man of many questions.

78

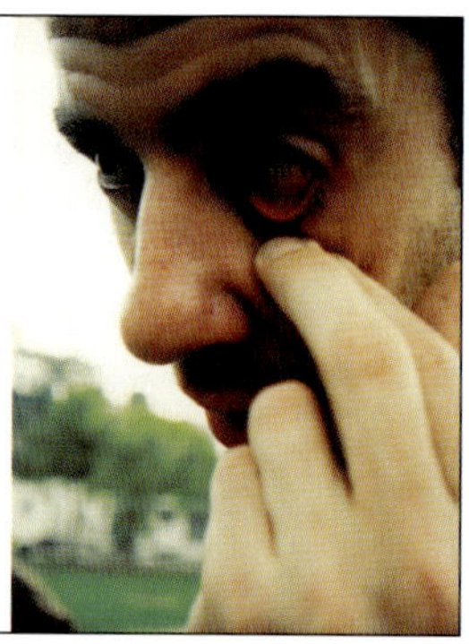

80

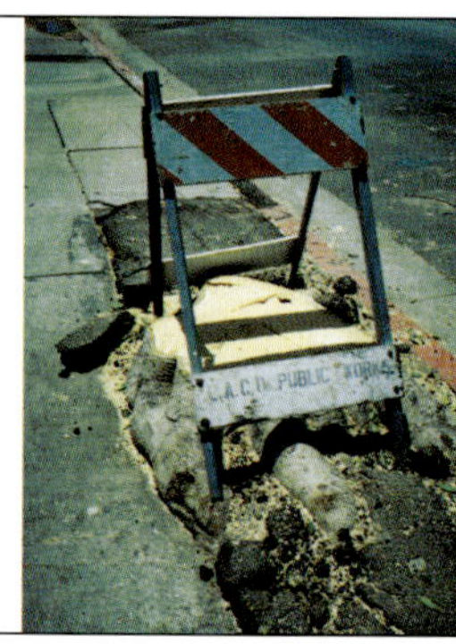

82

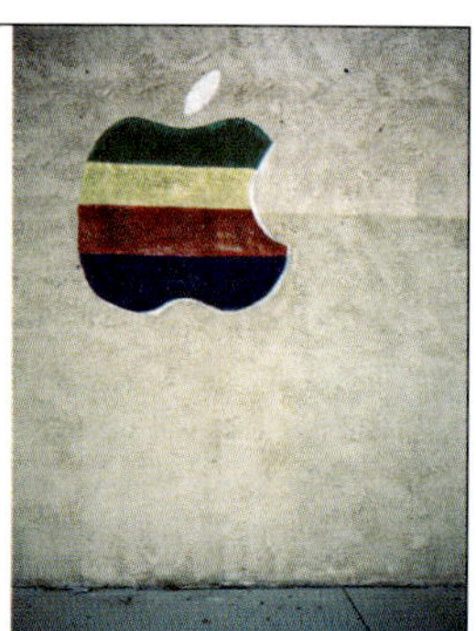

84

Spencer Fujimoto
Spencer's one of those dudes who you're never quite sure if he's East coast or West coast. I used to think he was East coast, then I thought he was West coast, but then he went East coast on me again. In the end I guess it doesn't really matter.

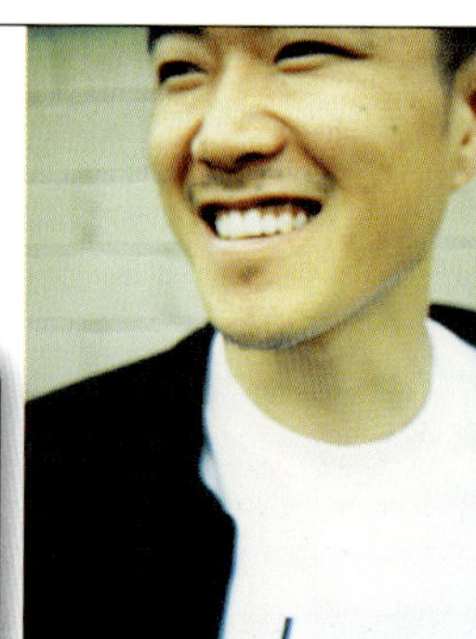

86

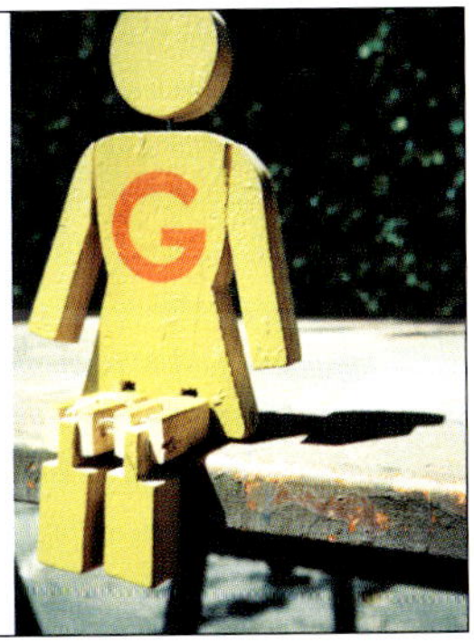

Eric Koston
There's a certain uncomfortable phase that Eric's locks go through whenever he grows them out. The phase is called "The Wig" and it's what you're looking at here.

88

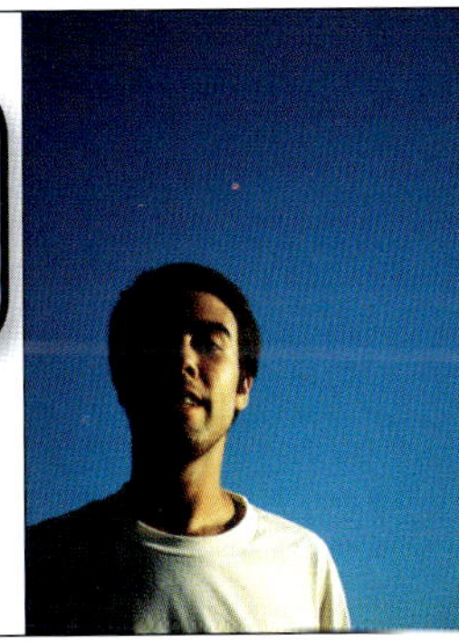

90

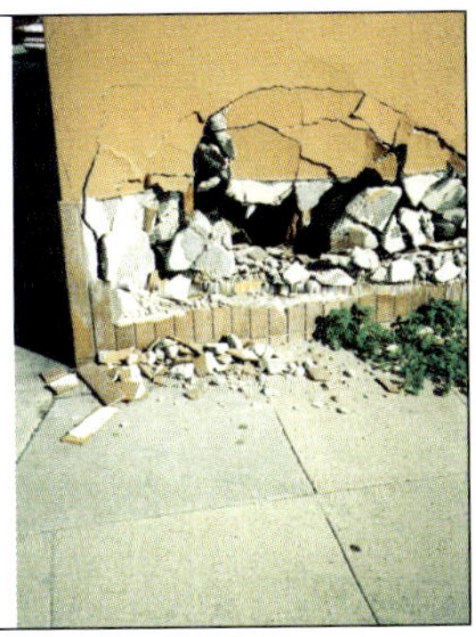

92

Chico Brenes
Next time you see Chico ask him about the time he got his appendix removed in South America and wound up with a scar that looks like he got all of his organs removed then re-inserted. Gnarly.

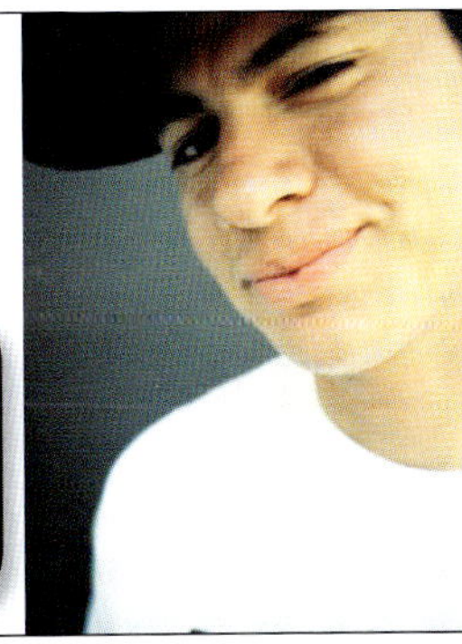

94

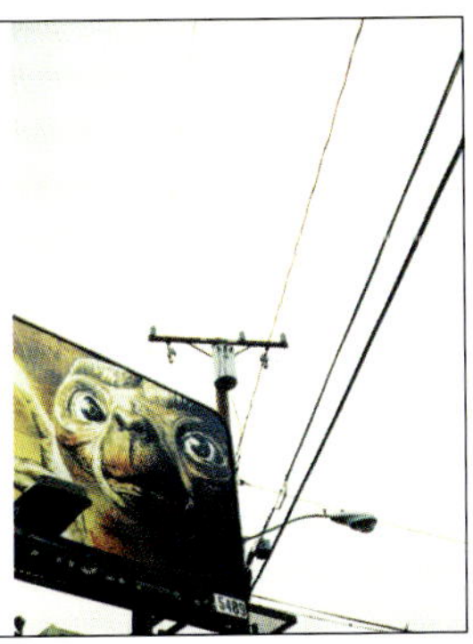

Marc Johnson
This is a poached shot from the set of Marc's first Lakai ad shoot. I think he was trying to say something about corporate affairs in skateboarding with the pig mask but I could be wrong.

96

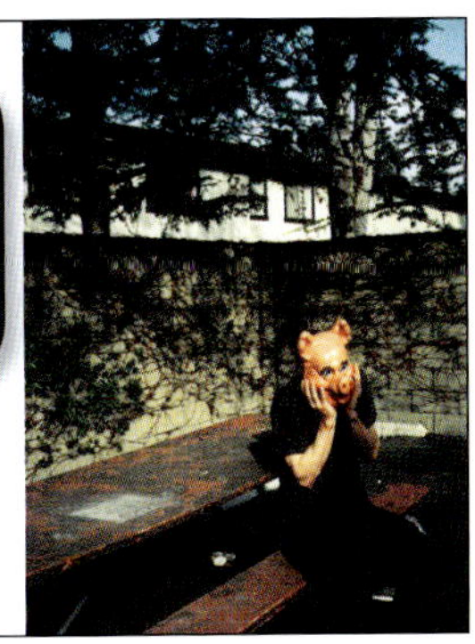

98

Marc Johnson
Another poached shot from the same Lakai ad shoot. No political statement, just a '70s basketball getup.

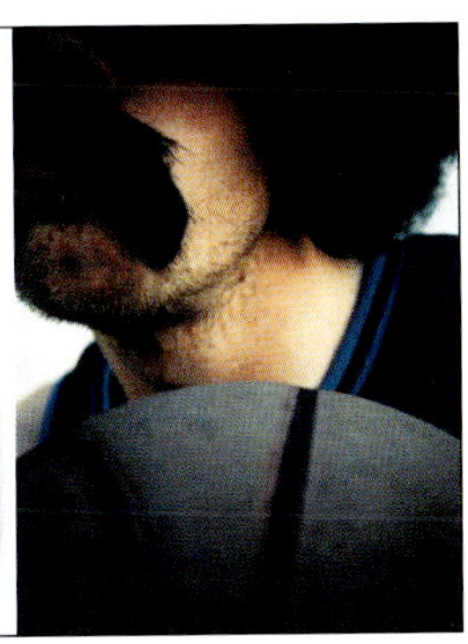

100

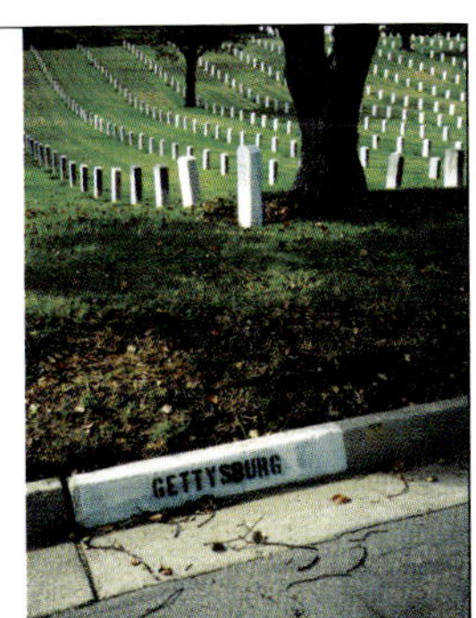

Guy Mariano

Guy is one of those mysterious Tom Penny-esque characters that rabid skate fans always ask you questions about if you work for Girl. In the three years that I worked there I only saw the dude twice, so please don't ask me about him because I have no idea.

102

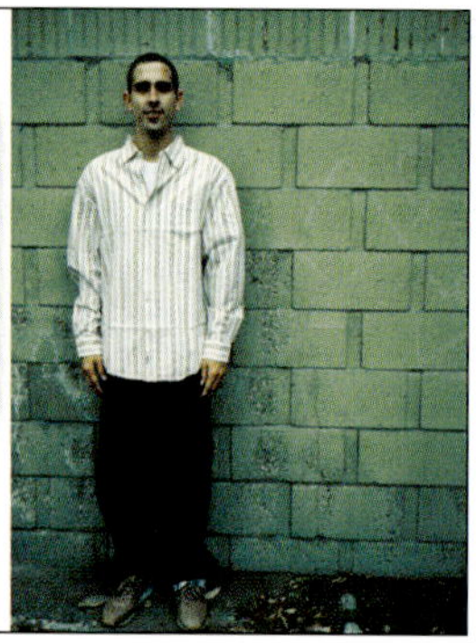

104

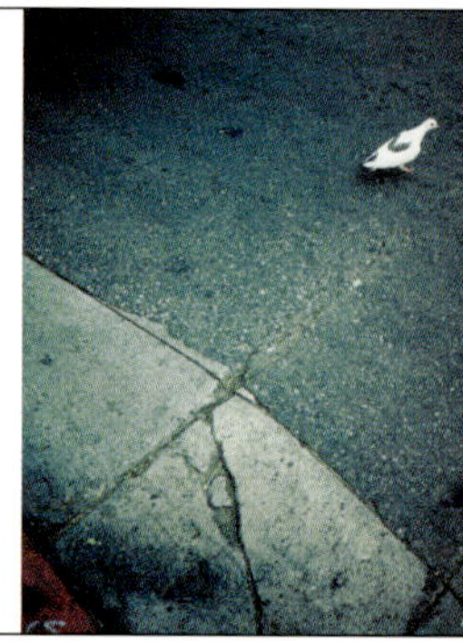

Rodrigo TX

I've looked at this photo a hundred times yet I still can't tell if Rodrigo's giving the camera a gangster face or if he was giving me a "hurry up and take the picture, asshole" face.

106

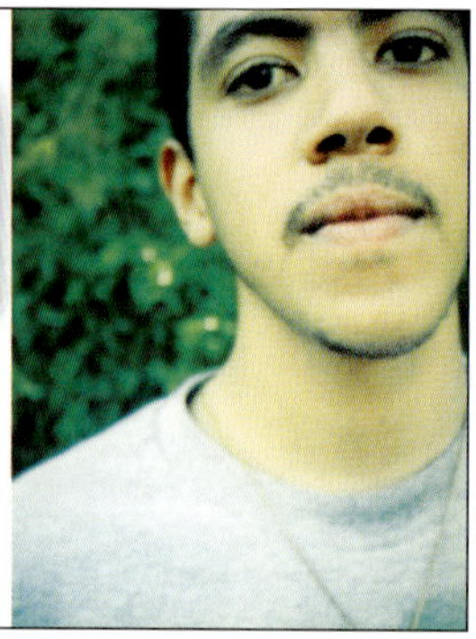

108

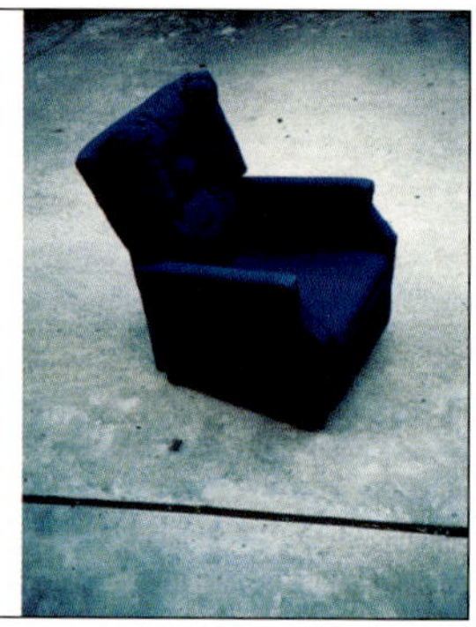

110

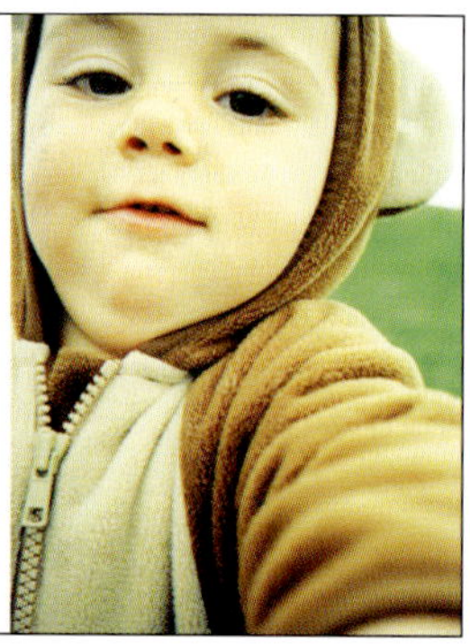

112

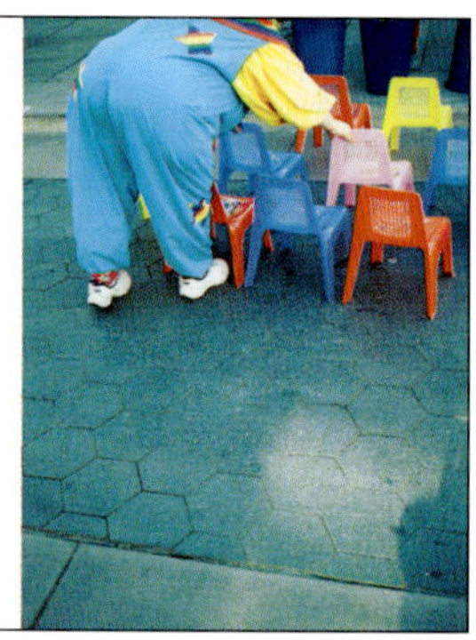

114

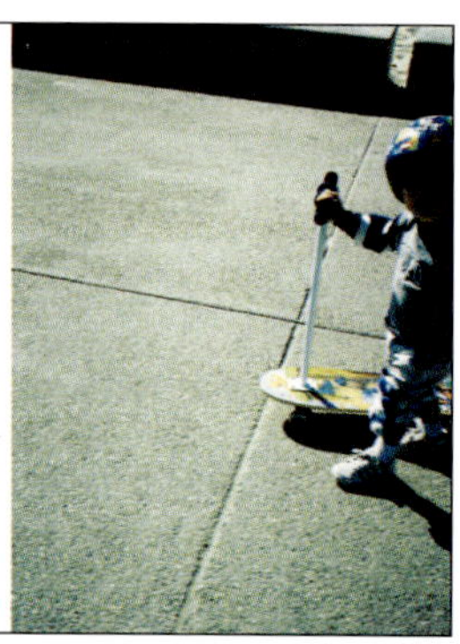

116

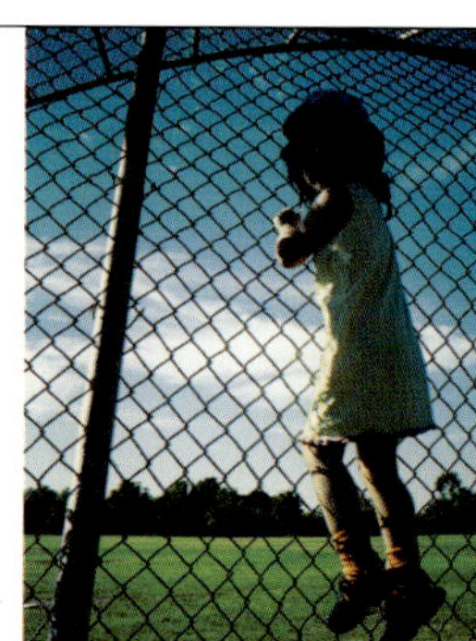

118

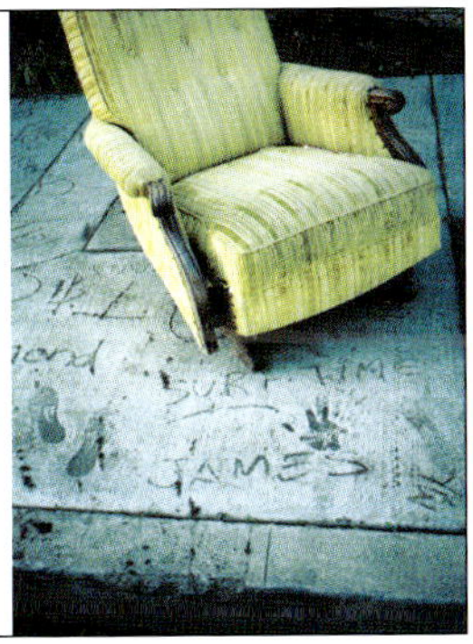

120

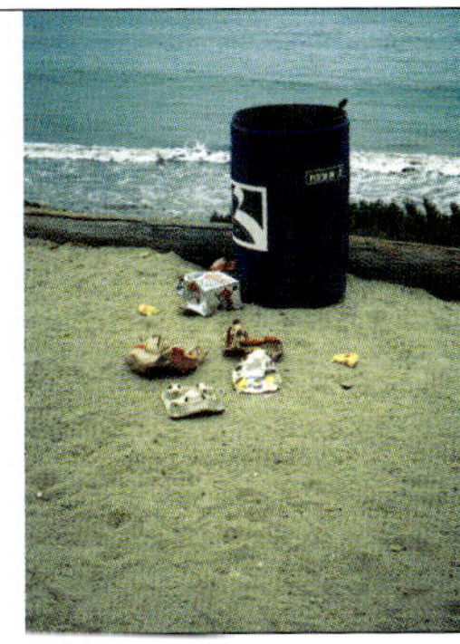

122

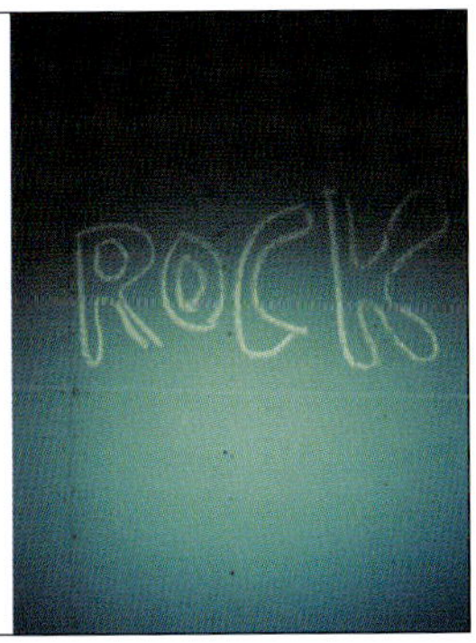

124

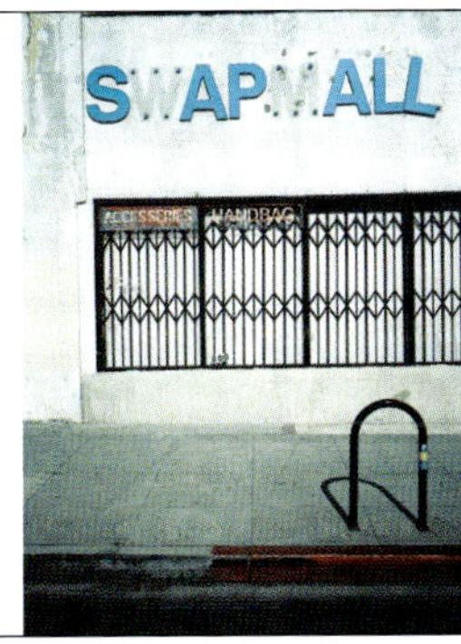

126

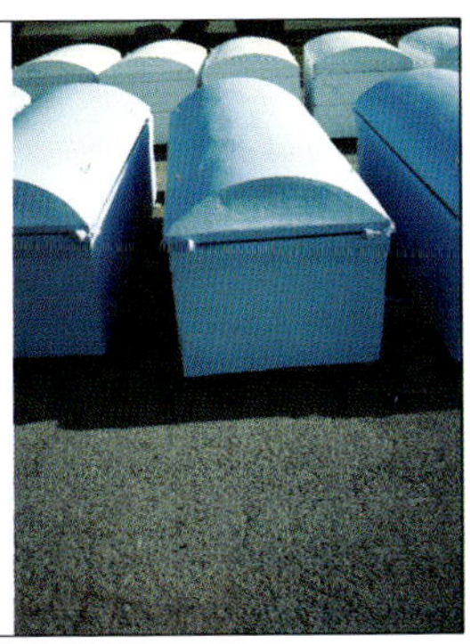

Jason Dill
The last time I saw Dill he showed me a journal of his that had a scab taped into it as well as a bunch of thoughts put down on paper. It was pretty rad. The dude is rad.

128

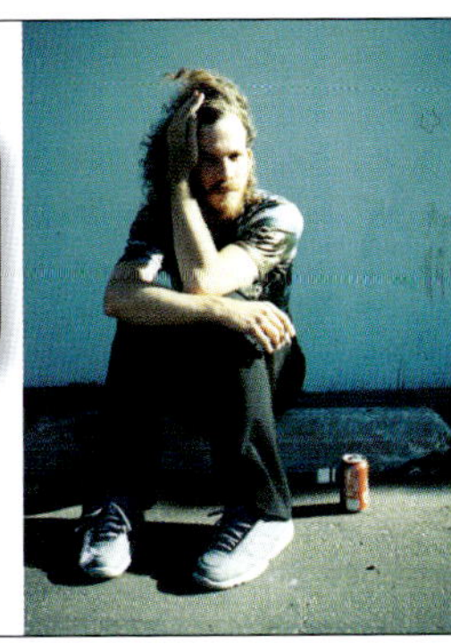

130

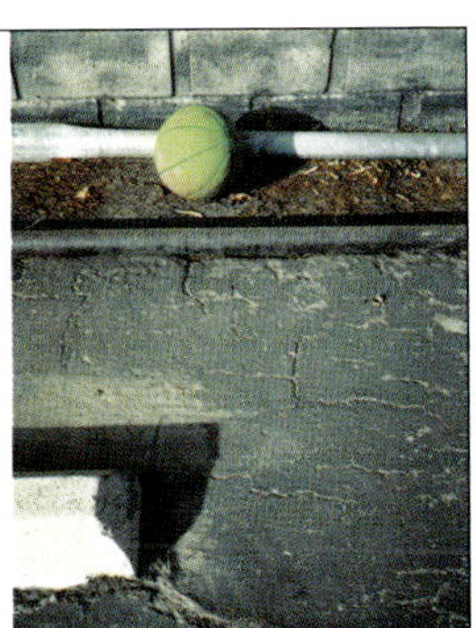

Eric Koston
Griptape art by Froston.

132

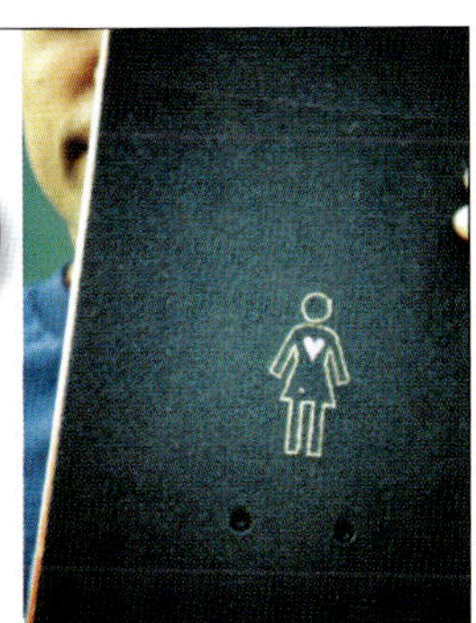

134

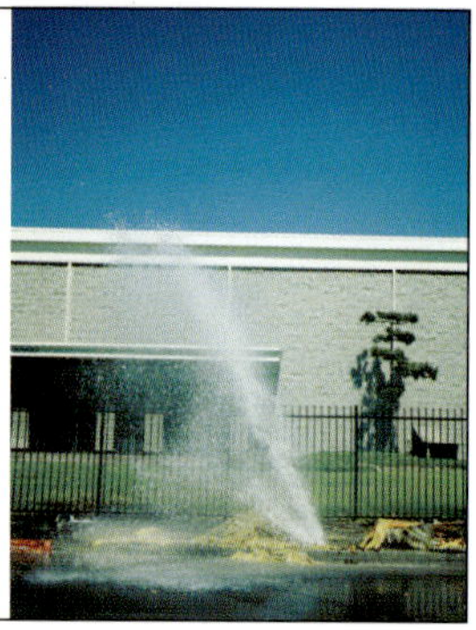

Steve Berra and Eric Koston
This could be a photo of Joe Dingleberry and Adam McKnackleson's feet but it's actually Eric and Steve. Seriously. I promise.

136

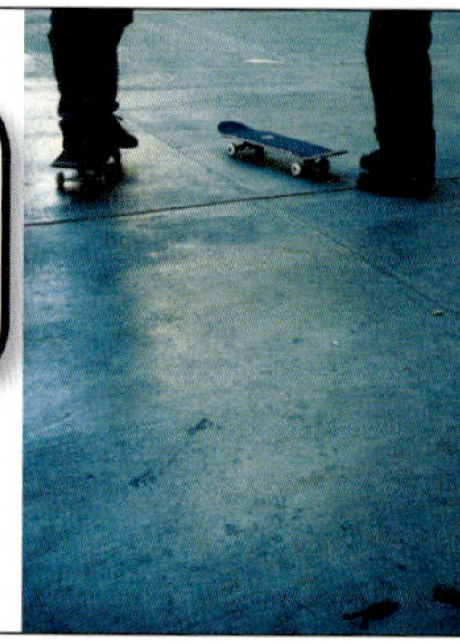

138

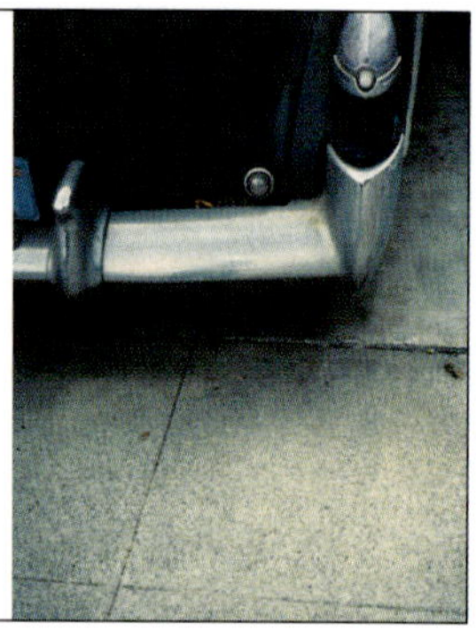

140

Lance Mountain
Much like Kenny, Lance is a genuine dude and every time I see him I'm reminded of that fact. This photo was shot immediately following Rodrigo's gangster face/"shoot the photo, asshole" photo.

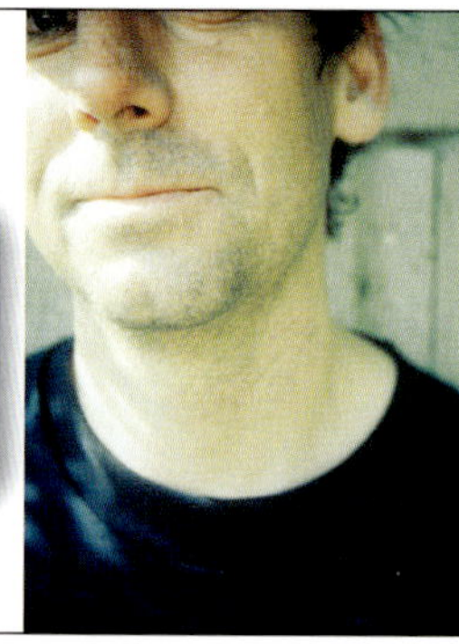

142

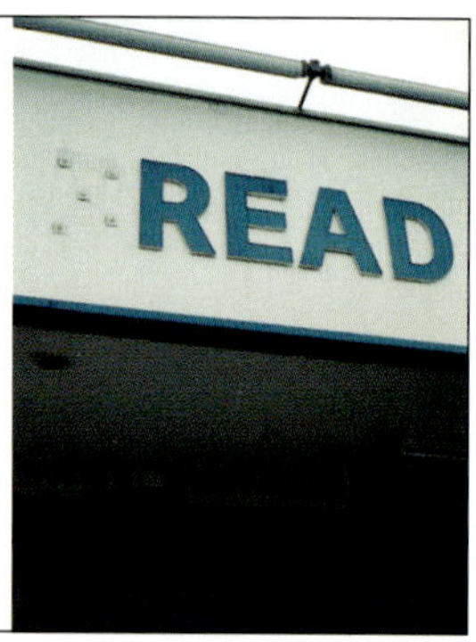

144

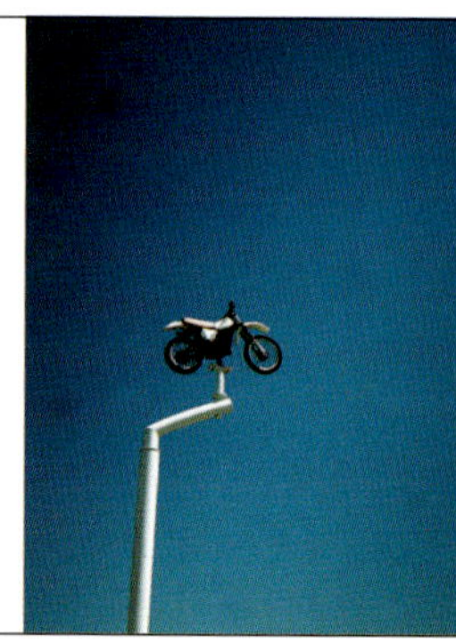

146

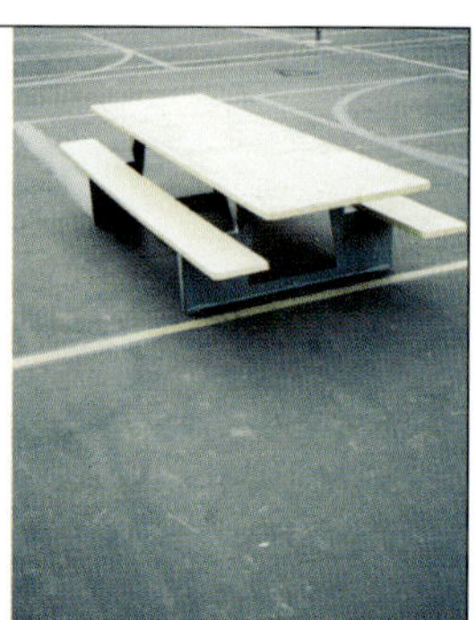

148

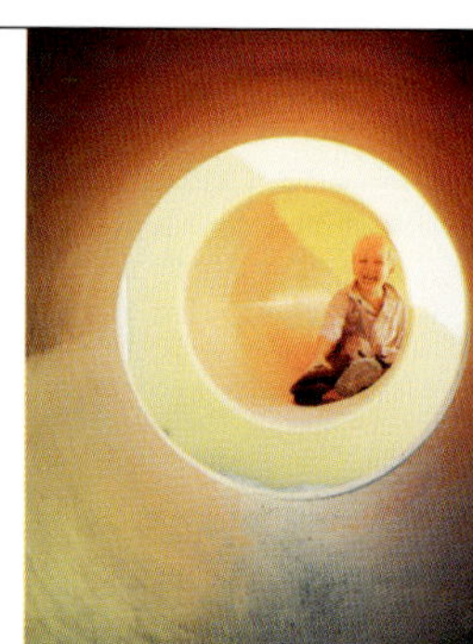

Ty Evans
Ty's one of those dudes who gives you knuckles or a high five and you're secretly like "Damn, that hurt" because he's so enthusiastic about it. Much like his videos, his energy is unrivaled.

150

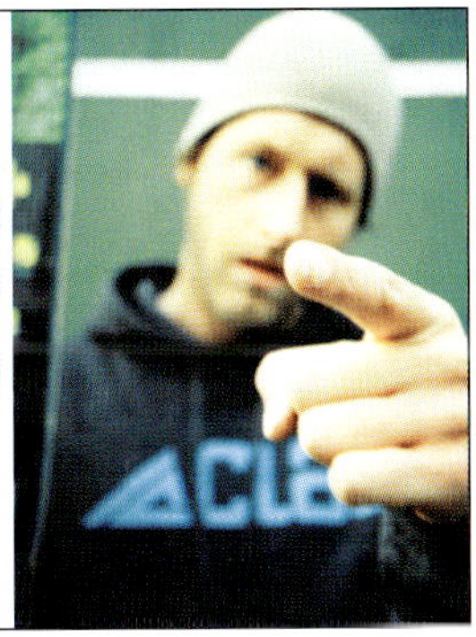

152

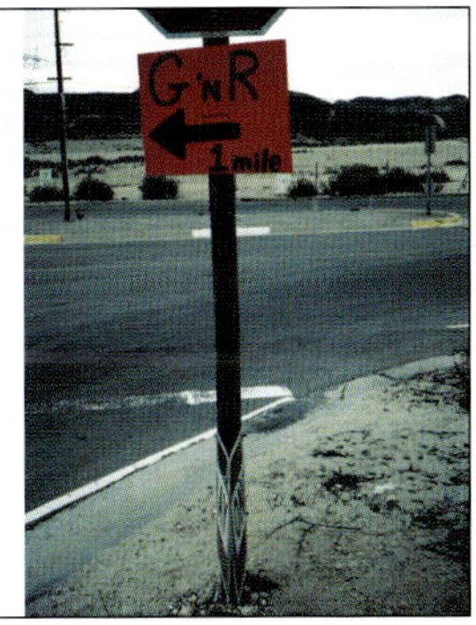

154

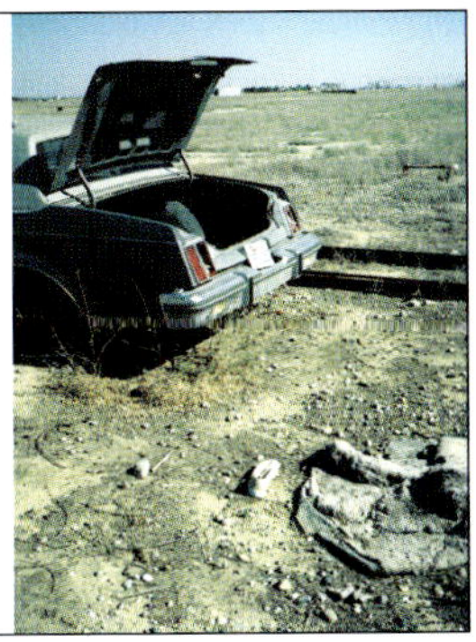

Mike Carroll
Here we have Mike Carroll posing in front of a throw up he did. Just kidding.

156

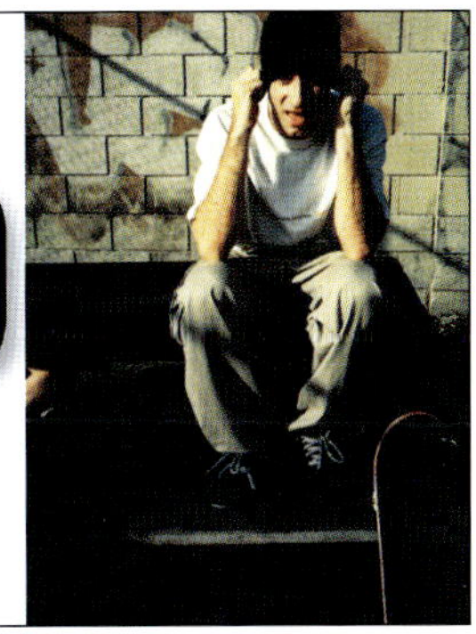

158

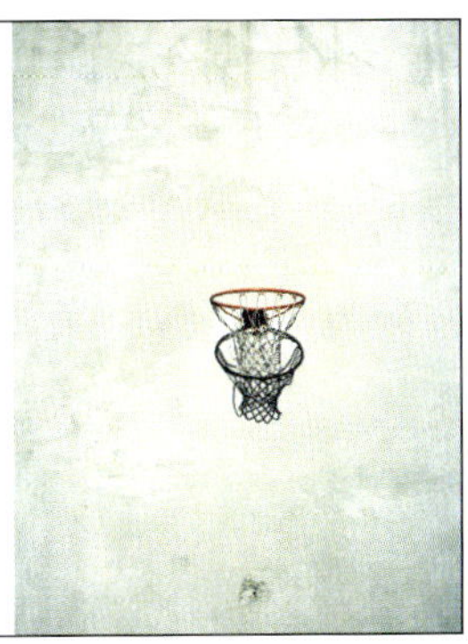

160

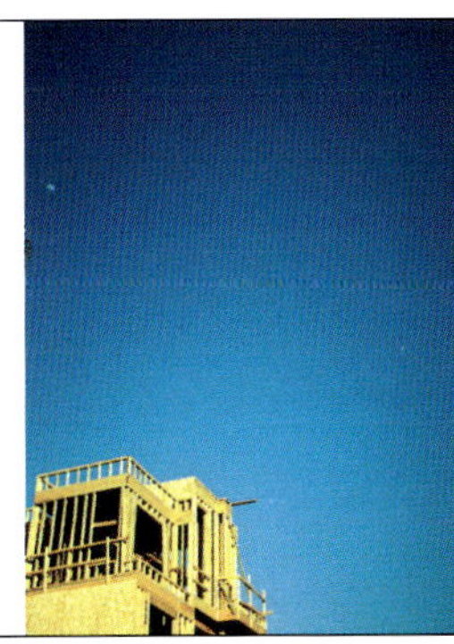

162

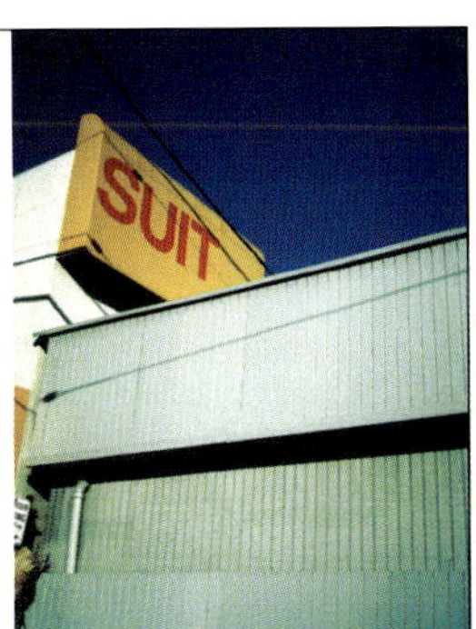

164

glass